FLU SELF-DEFENCE

Stimulating Immunity with TCM

Wei Huiqiang

FOREIGN LANGUAGES PRESS

First Edition 2010

ISBN 978-7-119-06130-6

FOREWORD

In the face of a serious global influenza pandemic, people cannot help but ask whether the virus is unconquerable, or whether the thinking, policies and measures relating to prevention and treatment are perhaps wrong. Research findings indicate the latter. The conventional approaches to flu prevention are over-focused on the virus but fail to mobilize the body's innate adaptability and immunity (known and latent) to fight infection.

Currently, in Chinese medical circles and overseas, there is great room for improvement in combating flu. In addition to vaccination and medication, many scientific approaches call for focus on stimulating known and latent ability for self-healing and improving self-immunity, in particular improving microcirculation of the respiratory system.

The New Century Medical Model and the New TCM Anti-Flu Therapy are both theoretically and practically innovative, from lab experiment through to clinical application. They supplement what is lacking in conventional measures and are easy, effective, "green," and inexpensive to popularize. Embodying the TCM concept of "preventative treatment," the new therapy aims to activate the body's known and latent resistance, and conforms to the TCM principles of "strengthening what is healthy and dispelling the pathogenic" and "when there is sufficient healthy *qi* inside, pathogens have no way to invade the body."

At the same time as focusing on the virus, one ought to also emphasize stimulating the body's known and latent resistance. Wei Huiqiang points out that flu prevention therapy should combine fighting the virus and activating the body's own resistance; should combine infection surveillance with immunotherapy, pharmacotherapy and non-pharmacotherapy, integrate exogenous measures (e.g. vaccination, medication and non-medication therapies) with the endogenous (e.g. physical exercises such as *daoyin*). Medical training has been organized in several centers for the application and popularization of the all-new approach. It encompasses moxibustion, massage, cupping, hot salt-pack compress, hot air treatment, and *daoyin*, plus a set of scientific innovations, simple ways of increasing immune strength, in particular by improving the microcirculation and health of the respiratory system. In clinical practice it has met with praise from the public, medical experts and academics.

The New TCM Anti-Flu Therapy follows the principles of the New Century Medical Model and is more holistic, economical, easier and safer than conventional measures, as well as being very practicable. It is also a full expression of the concepts of "putting people first" and "harmony between man and nature," perfectly integrated in Chinese preventive medicine and health preserving medicine.

The holistic approach of the New Century Medical Model is applicable for the prevention and treatment of H1N1 Flu as well as other viral epidemics. TCM non-pharmacotherapy is virtually cost-free, easily learned, and deserving of popularization on a wide scale.

CONTENTS

Chapter 1

OVERVIEW OF THE NEW TCM ANTI-FLU THERAPY

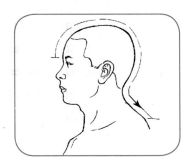

1.1 A New Era in the Fight Against Flu

The key to defeating influenza and the pursuit of health and beauty are quests shared by all mankind. The responsibility for opening up a new era in the fight against flu has fallen to the world of medicine and science.

Scientific research has established the following facts: the average human brain weighs 1360 gm; it is the result of over 500 million years of vertebrate evolution; and it is the most advanced and sophisticated instrument in the universe. A human brain contains 20 billion nerve cells (or neurons), but we utilize only a small amount of them. This indicates that there remains much scope for activating its vast potential to make our lives more fulfilled, healthy and pleasant, specifically in areas such as winning out against flu by stimulating and harnessing the body's own resistance.

The new therapy detailed in the following pages is an easy, effective and scientific way to mobilize innate immunity. It opens up the way to defeating flu, and is a natural and effective approach to health, beauty and youthfulness into the bargain.

1.2 Brief History of the New Therapy

The New TCM Anti-Flu Therapy is rooted deep in history. Many records attest to the ancient origins of its related massage, acupuncture and *daoyin* exercises.

Yoga, for health maintenance, anti-aging and beauty, originated in India some five millennia ago. Chinese massage therapy was present even in primitive society. It is said that over 4,600 years ago, Yu Fu, a minister of the Yellow Emperor, built on his ancestors' experience to pioneer the "ancient eight massage therapies;" namely, mediating, tonifying *qi*, kneading and pinching, activating collaterals, pushing and pressing, dispelling, relieving rigidity, and clenching teeth. Stories about Yu Fu's practice of massage were recorded in *Records of the Historian: Memoirs of Masters Bian Que and Cang Gong, Garden of Anecdotes,* and *Han Ying's Illustrations of the Didactic Application of the Classic of Songs.* Through years of research and practice, the author has proved the efficacy of some of these ancient massage therapies in preventing, treating and recovering from flu, as well as in beauty and health maintenance.

The Yellow Emperor's Classics of Internal Medicine, written over 2,000 years ago, is the earliest extant medical canon. The book systematically elaborated on the theory of "essence, *qi* and spirit," which lie at the heart of TCM therapy for flu prevention, health and beauty, providing a theoretical basis for massage practice as well as the new self-applied therapy in the above areas.

In the Qin and Han dynasties, massage became a major treatment method and professional masseurs emerged. At that time, massage was mainly used to treat "cold and heat caused by flaccid syncope," "obstruction of collateral channels," "rigidity of limbs" and "muscle rigidity" caused by cold-damp (cited from "Plain Questions: On the Regulation of Collateral Channels," a part of *The Yellow Emperor's Classics of Internal Medicine*) and aches caused by "retention of cold-*qi* between the intestines and stomach and below interior-exterior interspace" (cited from "Plain Questions: On Aches"). Medical writings on massage also appeared during this period, for example "Ten-volume Discourse on Massage between the Yellow Emperor and Qi Bo" extracted from *Han History: Record of Art and Culture* which was probably China's first monograph on massage. Sadly, it no longer survives.

The *Daoyin Exercise Chart* unearthed from the Han tombs at Mawangdui in Changsha, Hunan, introduces various body and limb movements; the bamboo book *Ten Questions*, also from Mawangdui, says "regulation of *qi* through concentration of mind so as to see and hear well, make skin glow, smoothen meridians, and nourish *yin*." These are all supportive evidence for the long history of TCM in flu prevention, self health-building and beauty.

From then on, flu prevention, health preservation and beauty building became more popular. In the time of the Three Kingdoms (220-280), Hua Tuo pioneered the "Five-Animal Exercise" for disease prevention, bodybuilding, beauty treatment and health preservation. In the Wei, Jin, Sui and Tang dynasties (from the third to the 10th century), massage became a specialist field and medical masseurs appeared. Medical writings in this field in this time include "Ten Chapters of Classics on *Daoyin* and Massage" in *Baopuzi: The Internal — Broad View* by Ge Hong of the Jin Dynasty (265-420), and *Treatise on the Causes and Symptoms of Diseases* compiled by Chao Yuanfang and others of the Sui Dynasty (581-618). In the latter, most symptoms have accompanying related health therapies. For instance, the section on face and body self-massage therapy for cold and heat-generated headache provides a lively and accurate description of the effects and mechanisms of this self-massage, and is inspiring for flu prevention and health preservation.

10

In modern times, flu prevention and treatment advanced further along with health and beauty building. Plenty of medical writings in the field emerged, but were despised, marginalized or even destroyed by the ruling class, and thus spread only among the common people. After the founding of New China in 1949, thanks to the Central Government's valuing of China's traditional medical heritage and the health care of its people, there has been a flourishing of massage, acupuncture, moxibustion and *daoyin* exercises, yielding brilliant results. Although at one point, ultra-left thinking led to the dismissal of massage and beauty therapy as legacies of capitalism, acupuncture, moxibustion and *daoyin* were energetically developed and even gradually aroused international attention for their own practical values.

With the rapid development of modern science, many emergent subjects and high technologies have been applied to various fields. The New TCM Anti-Flu Therapy attempts to make use of modern research findings guided by contemporary medical theories, namely cybernetics, System Theory, Information Theory, Microcirculation Theory, holistic biomedicine and human aging studies. It is also a scientific and systematic trial application of the precious TCM legacy in the areas of flu prevention, self health-building and beauty.

1.3 Exploring the Mechanism of the New TCM Health Therapy

The New TCM Health Therapy for Flu Prevention and Treatment maximizes and activates immunity by means of special Eastern techniques of health and beauty, techniques that are effective in preventing flu and in achieving health, beauty and longevity. The mechanism is complex, whether viewed from the standpoint of TCM or Western medical theory, or in the light of modern research findings. Here, an initial exploration of just three aspects is outlined.

TCM Theory

1) Harmonize *yin* and *yang*, balance the five elements. The therapy clears meridian and collateral channels by acupoint massage so as to harmonize *yin* and *yang*, balance the five elements and promote harmony between the *zang* organs (heart, liver, spleen, lung, kidney, pericardium) and the *fu* organs (small intestine, large intestine, gall bladder, urinary bladder, stomach), and between *ying* (nutrition) and *wei* (defence). The smooth flow of *qi* and blood nourishes the whole body and maintains the normal function of all organs and tissues, thereby enhancing the body's immunity to flu.

2) Dredge meridian and collateral channels and smoothen joint movement. The therapy unblocks the collateral channels, strengthens muscles and bones, moves *qi* and activates blood, and smoothens joint movements so as to build "flexibility of the body and harmony of *qi* flow."

3) Strengthen the primary and the healthy, replenish and supplement the original *qi*. As an old saying goes, "The three treasures of heaven are the sun, moon and stars, while the three treasures of the human body are *jing* essence, *qi* and *shen* spirit." Among the three treasures of the human body, essence is the foundation, *qi* the driving force and spirit the controller, all of them fundamental to health and beauty and in preventing flu. The new therapy stresses replenishing the essence, *qi* and spirit in the

body, in other words "supplementing congenital *qi*." For example, therapies like "strengthening essence," "supplementing essence," "promoting longevity," "anti-aging treatment," "nourishing *yin*," and "building beauty" are all effective for flu prevention.

Modern Medical Theory

1) Through positive treatment input by physical stimulation (e.g. unblocking meridian and collateral channels through acupoint massage), the therapy activates a series of responses through neural segmental reflex and the reaction and feedback of abdominal organs. These reflexes work directly on endocrine organs or indirectly through the nervous system, thus regulating the functions of nerves, body fluids and endocrine organs.

For instance, under optimal stimulation, the cerebral cortex can coordinate its functional units to work harmoniously (in order), and ensure the right level of secretions, thus improving blood circulation and nourishing body organs.

Persistent practice of the therapy will gradually raise the practitioner's level of health, beauty and fitness and innate ability to prevent and overcome flu.

2) Through neural reflexes, the self-applied therapy stimulates inactive histamine in tissues to release active histamine and acetylcholine. Thus, it boosts blood circulation and lymphatic circulation, improves metabolism, and activates the optimal elements in respiratory, digestive, urinary, reproductive, muscular, nervous, and endocrine systems. All of this is conducive to flu prevention, general health and beauty.

3) The therapy acts upon blood flow dynamics to cause temporary blood redistribution; increases red blood cells, white blood cells, platelets and hemoglobin; improves the phagocytic ability of white cells and serum complement titer. It also improves the stress response to nociceptive stimulus by hypophysis cerebri, adrenal cortex system, sympathetic nerves and adrenal medullary system. Furthermore, it improves the body's immunity (at cellular and molecular levels). The strengthening of internal organic vitality promotes the recovery of damaged tissues and harmonizes the internal power of the body, thus achieving flu prevention and health building.

4) Psychologically, the therapy arouses a pleasant feeling, which helps to ward off worry, anxiety and negativity, simultaneously increasing the courage to overcome difficulties and the confidence to pursue health and beauty. Practice has proven that emotions do influence health and can also affect active personal involvement in flu prevention and building health. Therefore, maintaining mental calm and pleasant emotions is beneficial in this regard.

5) "Life lies in movement" is a well known saying. The physical exercises introduced in this new TCM health therapy also help to build up a healthy body.

6) "Use and disuse," a fundamental principle in biology, also finds full expression in this health therapy. Persistent practice, in the proper sequence, progressing from quantity to quality of movements, increases the body's resistance to flu.

Modern Research Findings
1) Biocybernetics. The current opinion of international life science

experts is that from the viewpoint of cybernetics, the human body is a complete self-coordinating system with the brain as its center. The brain analyzes and processes information from inside and outside the body so as to maintain its dynamic balance. The new Eastern self-massage therapy works by giving optimal stimulus to the nerve center through gentle, constant and mild physical stimulus, so as to relax the cerebral cortex and the body and achieve a new dynamic balance through the body's own self-coordinating system. The fundamental basis of the therapy is to act via the body's homeostatic mechanism and immunity, and is thus in accordance with life science principles.

2) Psychosomatic medicine. Psychosomatic Homeostasis Theory is an advanced life science and has aroused extraordinary interest in the international scientific community. The therapy introduced in the book embodies the principle of "body and mind as one" which also conforms to that of modern psychosomatic medicine.

3) System Internal Energy. The imbalance of any human body system will cause pathological changes that will surely result in system disturbance. The therapy to be introduced in this book can adjust the imbalanced body system, and thereby maintain health and beauty and improve flu resistance. For instance, by practicing this therapy, a patient with the syndrome of blood stasis due to *qi* stagnation, will increase his system internal energy and accelerate the flowing of *qi* and blood. By activating blood and regulating *qi*-moving, the therapy is beneficial to beauty and health and improves the body's immunity to influenza.

4) Information Theory. Modern biological research findings reveal that each of the abdominal organs contains its distinct bio-information

(frequency and biological electricity). If there is any pathological change in an internal organ, its bio-information will change, and this will affect the balance of the whole body system. Through proper optimal stimulus or energy transmission, this therapy acts on certain parts of the body (or acupoints) to produce certain biological information. The information is sent to related abdominal organs through the body's transmission system, adjusts the previous imbalanced information, and promotes the reconstruction of a new dynamic balance. Through bio-information adjustment, the therapy is thus effective for health preservation, beauty building and flu prevention.

5) Microcirculation Theory. Microcirculation specialists believe that effective microcirculatory function of a body ensures the maintenance of normal physiological and functional information. Diseases occur when microcirculation is obstructed. The health building skills introduced in this therapy are effective in regulating microcirculation of the body. For example, rub your hands till they are warm and then massage your face. This will raise facial skin temperature and boost facial blood circulation, thus achieving the effects of health preservation and flu prevention.

6) Aging mechanism. Mental, physiological, environmental and social factors all affect senescence, but the process starts with the cells (in particular the important cerebral neurons), which results in metabolic imbalance. This health therapy effectively improves the metabolism, with multiple benefits for health, beauty, longevity and flu resistance.

In conclusion, since the mechanism of the new TCM therapy is truly complex, much remains to be discussed on this subject.

1.4 Main Features of the New Therapy

Health and Beauty Benefits
The Therapy is fundamentally different from previous flu, beauty and health building treatments. Ordinary health and beauty routines cannot compare with its multiple functions — e.g. nerve relaxation, mood stabilization, adjustment of body, mind and internal organs. It introduces the unique Eastern practice of *daoyin*. It unveils the secrets of self health and beauty care. It also combines the essence of ancient *qigong*'s prophylactic and curative effects, yoga, and meridian massage techniques with all their benefits for health and beauty. Its features include:

Combination of Body and Mind
To practice the Therapy, one needs to concentrate the mind, eliminate all distracting thoughts, combine body and mind, will and spirit, externality and internality, motion and stillness, and more importantly, mind, body and the circulation of *qi*. Normally take five to seven deep breaths, then concentrate on using the thoughts of self-activated care to eliminate all distractions, so that the mind is centered, the breath is stable, the thoughts focused on performing the exercise or movement, thereby benefiting the Therapy's efficacy.

Beauty and Health in One
No matter how expensive one's cosmetics, or however skilled the beautician, they can only bring about external beauty. They cannot effect qualitative change or bring a sparkle to lifeless eyes. But by practicing this Therapy, not only can your eyes begin to glow; flu prevention, brow care, beauty and health preservation come as part of the package.

Combined Measures

The Therapy can be practiced on its own, or combined with other treatments for flu, beauty and health preservation. It can increase the effectiveness of flu prevention and treatment and reduce the side effects of medication. As we all know, meticulous make-up with expensive cosmetics is never a match for light make-up on a healthy complexion. Because the Therapy combines qualitative advantages — increasing vital energy and blood, keeping internal organs healthy, exercising muscles, smoothing skin and reducing wrinkles — the addition of cosmetics can make you more radiant and alluring.

Self-applied Health Preservation

The Therapy teaches practitioners to grasp a new, Eastern approach to preventing flu. Improvement in general health and flu resistance can be achieved through one's own hands, without assistance.

Easy and Convenient

Practitioners need only to be clear about their needs, select appropriate exercise and practice accordingly. No other medical devices and drugs are needed to reach their goal.

Remarkable Results

The Therapy can be helpful in many disorders, such as chronic bronchitis, rhinitis, neck and shoulder syndrome, and the common cold. It can also strengthen the practitioner's body and is beneficial to increasing flu immunity.

Extensive Application Range

The Therapy has rich content and extensive application range. It can be utilized not only in preventative, clinical and rehabilitation medicine, it also has a bright future in cosmetic medicine, health preservation medicine and public health medicine.

Flexibility
Practitioners can select relevant chapters according to their individual priorities.

The World's Only Endogenous Therapy
Daoyin therapy is an internal prophylactic and curative exercise, and features prominently in the Therapy.

Safe and without Side Effects
The Therapy will be effective provided it is carried out according to the rules. It is a safe, environment-friendly therapy established on the basis of TCM. It is non-toxic and without side effects.

1.5 Points to Note

Practitioners should take note of the following:
- Fresh air: the Therapy can be practiced at home in a clean, quiet environment, with fresh air and suitable room temperature. Avoid draughts.
- Fingernails: The nails should be trimmed and items such as rings removed, to avoid hindering the practice or damaging the skin.
- Clean warm hands: The hands should be clean and warm (especially during facial practice), to avoid muscle tension or adverse effects when touching the skin (especially during facial practice). Wash hands in warm water before starting.
- Accurate location of acupoints: This massage method achieves its effect by stimulating the acupoints. Therefore accurate location

of these points is very important. See the illustrations for location guidance.

- Appropriate strength: The use of strength will affect the results. Insufficient strength will not be enough to stimulate the acupoints, but excessive strength might result in injury. Usually one starts light and progresses to heavy, gradually reverting to light at the end. If practicing according to the rules, a faint prickling sensation is normal.

- Flexible choice: Practice content can be selected according to one's specific health condition, lifestyle, and requirements as regards flu, health and beauty. There is no need for strict adherence to the order in this book.

- Step by step: Start off with a few routines and gradually increase the number. Sudden increases should be avoided. As your body adjusts, the number and intensity of the routines can be increased in easy stages.

- Perseverance is the key: Perseverance is indispensable. A fine start and poor finish will certainly not achieve ideal results.

- In acute cases first consult a doctor: In the case of an acute disease, one should first check with a clinic before choosing whether to practice this method. This will benefit recovery.

1.6 Common Techniques of the Therapy

The Therapy and self-massage treatment are easy to carry out. It is important to accompany them with breath adjustment. The common manipulation methods are categorized as follows:

1. Pressing
Definition: A massage technique involving rhythmic pressing with the hands on the appropriate acupoints (or part).

Action: Using wrist strength, press and manipulate in rhythmic, smooth movements, with appropriate breathing. The strength should gradually progress from light to heavy and then back to light, the degree of strength depending on which part of the body is involved. It should be felt quite obviously, and sometimes there will be a tingling sensation.

Common categories: Finger pressing (Fig.1), palm pressing (Fig.2), single-hand pressing, double-hand pressing.

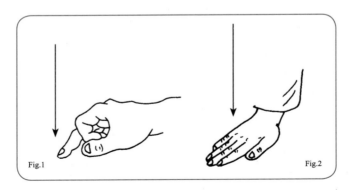

Fig.1 Fig.2

Functions: TCM believes that pressing has the effect of unblocking the channels, relieving pain, helping digestion and improving the skin. In the view of modern medical research, pressing can relax and adjust muscles. Some people believe that pressing and rubbing in combination can bring down high-level nerve excitement, improve blood movement and nutrition of tissues, strengthen oxygenation, and change stasis within the lymphatic vessels.

2. Circular Rubbing

Definition: A massage technique involving placing the hands on the appropriate acupoints (or part), and moving them with a gentle circular rubbing action.

Action: Rub with the wrist strength, the movement should be light and coordinated. The strength of movement should be consistent. The frequency should not be too fast — normally 60 movements per minute. The massaged area should feel itchy and a little warm.

Common categories: Finger rubbing (Figs.3, 4), palm rubbing (Fig.5), single-hand rubbing, double-hand rubbing.

Functions: TCM believes that circular rubbing can regulate the

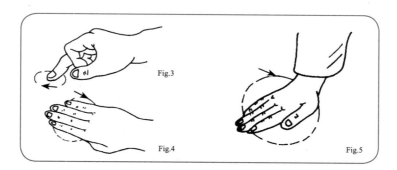

Fig.3

Fig.4

Fig.5

circulation of *qi*, promote digestion, diminish inflammation, reduce swelling, allay fever, regulate vital energy and the state of blood, alleviate pain, and improve skin condition. Some people believe that "quick rubbing is purging, slow rubbing is nourishing." Modern medicine believes that circular rubbing can improve sweat and sebaceous gland function, increase skin temperature, accelerate metabolism, regulate gastrointestinal peristalsis, enhance the circulation of blood and lymph. Some studies show that consistent circular rubbing for several minutes can lower excitement, relieve pain, and has an anesthetic effect.

3. Pushing

Definition: A massage technique in which steady, slow and even hand pressure is applied at the appropriate acupoint (or part) and pushed forward.

Action: Put hands flat against the skin, combining breath, push from the wrists, with rhythmic forward and backward movements. The forward push should not be too rapid or too strong, and the withdrawing movement should be very slow and gentle. The sensation will differ according to the strength exerted.

Common categories: Finger pushing (Fig.6), palm pushing (Fig.7), single-hand pushing, double-hand pushing.

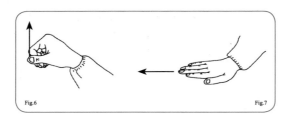

Fig.6   Fig.7

Functions: TCM theory believes that pushing can promote harmony between the nutritive *qi* and defensive *qi*, clear meridian channels, reduce swelling, arrest pain and improve skin conditions. Modern medical research shows that pushing can strengthen blood and lymph circulation, improve muscle ability, enhance nerve excitement and improve respiratory system function.

4. Grasping

Definition: A form of massage involving a grasping movement applied to the appropriate acupoint (or part).

Action: The movement is applied with finger strength, gripping and lifting skin and muscle. The seizing and loosening of the hold should be performed in series and gently with proper force, producing a sensation of distension and mild pain during the seizing, which is eased on release of the grip.

Common categories: Two-finger grasping (Fig.8), three-finger grasping (Figs.9, A, B), single-hand grasping, double-hand grasping.

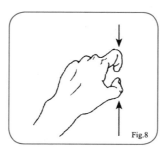

Fig.8

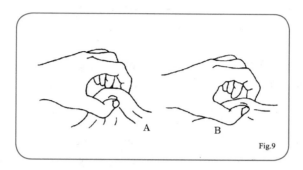

Fig.9

Functions: TCM theory believes that grasping massage can harmonize *yin* and *yang*, unblock meridian channels, dispel pathogenic wind and cold, relieve spasms and pain, promote blood circulation, and be used as first aid in cases of fainting. Modern medical study shows that grasping can restore feeling in the nerves, improve blood circulation, improve local metabolism, improve joint flexibility and muscle strength.

5. Tapping

Definition: A form of massage involving knocking with the hand (or suitable implement) on the appropriate acupoint (or part).

Action: The movement should be applied with wrist, progressing from light to heavy, and back to light (the recipient should feel relief) accompanied by "exhaling with a snort through the nose."

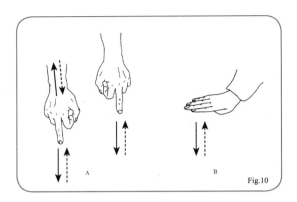

Fig.10

Movements should be easy, coordinated, flexible and rebounding, producing a penetrating and comfortable feeling.

Common categories: Finger knocking (Figs.10 A, B), fist knocking (Fig.11), single-hand knocking, double-hand knocking.

Functions: TCM believes that knocking can unblock meridian channels, dispel pathogenic wind cold and. promote blood and *qi* circulations. alleviate muscle ache, and improve body and skin conditions. Modern medical study shows that knocking can regulate neural activity, improve body fluid circulation, relieve pain, relax muscle tension, improve tissue nutrition and alleviate numbness and neurological disorder. Some people believe that knocking with medium force on the upper back can slow the pulse and can be helpful in treating arrhythmia.

6. Cross-pressing

Definition: A form of massage involving pressing at the appropriate acupoint (or part) with the fingers and moving horizontally.

26

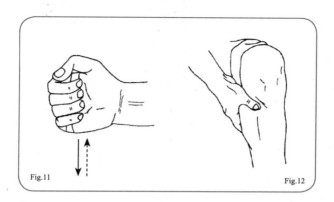

Fig.11   Fig.12

Action: Using the fingers with wrist strength to press evenly and steadily while moving in the direction perpendicular to the fiber and bone. It should produce a deep reaction, which then becomes one of comfort.

Common categories: Finger cross-pressing (Fig.12).
Functions: TCM believes that cross-pressing can dispel cold, sooth tendons to remove stasis, unblock meridian and collateral channels, alleviate fatigue and improve the complexion. In the view of modern medicine cross-pressing can improve local metabolism, adjust neurological state, and improve tissue oxygenation.

7. Rubbing
Definition: A form of massage involving moving the hands on the appropriate acupoint (or part) in back and forth movements (not circular).

Action: Press hand(s) flat against the skin with some pressure. Using wrist strength move forward and backward or side-to-side. The pressure should be even and appropriate, about 100 times per minute. It should produce a reaction of comfort and warmth.

Common categories: Palm rubbing (Fig.13), hypothenar rubbing, thenar eminence rubbing, single-hand rubbing, double-hand rubbing.

Functions: TCM believes that rubbing to and fro can dispel pathogenic wind and cold, promote the flow of *qi* and blood, improve spleen and stomach conditions, foster resistance to disease, dispel pathogenic influences, and improve body and skin conditions. Modern medicine believes that rubbing can raise local skin temperature, improve blood and lymph circulation and improve metabolism.

8. Kneading
Definition: A form of massage involving kneading with hands (or fingers) on the appropriate acupoint (or part).

Action: Move hands (or fingers) with the strength of the wrist (or palm) softly around the acupoint or part. The scale of movement is dependent on the acupoint or area to be treated. The hand(s)

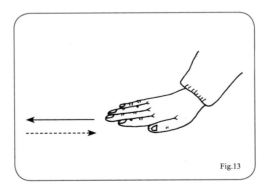

Fig.13

or finger(s) should remain in contact with the skin throughout the routine, so that the skin (connecting subcutaneous tissue) can move with the massage, which should usually be done in a rotating movement in a circular area. It should produce a response of evenness and deep comfort.

Common categories: Finger kneading (Fig.14), palm kneading (Fig.15), single-hand kneading and double-hand kneading.

Functions: TCM believes that kneading can improve the flow of *qi* and blood, reduce swelling and pain, improve spleen and stomach, unblock meridian channels, and improve body condition. Modern medical research shows that kneading can separate adhesions, increase histamine and acetylcholine in the tissues, improve flow of blood, body fluid circulation and tissue nutrition, and increase regeneration ability and disease resistance.

9. Twisting
Definition: A form of massage involving twisting with the fingers on the appropriate acupoint (or part).

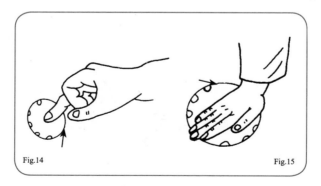

Fig.14　　　　　　　　　　　　　　　　Fig.15

Action: Applying wrist strength, use the fingertips and twist evenly, as if twisting thread. The pressure should be even and light (but not static). The movement should be quick, soft, continuous and natural. Initially it should produce a response of relaxation and itchiness, but once accustomed, the itchiness will disappear.

Common categories: Thumb-and-index-finger twisting (Fig.16), thumb-and-middle-finger twisting (Fig.17).

TCM believes that twisting can adjust *qi* and blood, improve articulation, reduce swelling and obstruction, reduce pain to induce sedation, dispel pathogenic wind, and improve body conditions. From the standpoint of modern medicine, twisting method can improve local metabolism, promote circulation and joint flexibility, and increase muscle strength. Some believe that twisting with short, light, low pressure and soft technique in the direction toward the heart can stimulate and nourish the body.

10. Pinching
Definition: A form of massage involving pinching with nails or finger tips on appropriate acupoints (or part).

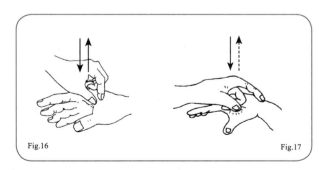

Fig.16   Fig.17

Action: Pinch lightly and appropriately with wrist strength. To avoid injury to skin and tissue, the movement should not be too heavy or quick. Strength of the pinching should be appropriate and it should produce deep comfort. Do not break the skin, but pinch marks may remain.

Common categories:Thumb-and-index-finger pinching (Fig.18), and thumb-and-middle-finger pinching (Fig.19).

Functions: TCM believes that pinching can unblock meridian channels, promote the flow of *qi* and blood, dispel pathogenic wind and cold, improve *ying* (nutrition) and *wei* (defence) systems, refresh and improve the function of the brain, relieve uneasiness and improve the skin. In the view of modern medicine the technique can reduce swelling, relieve pain, adjust nerve balance and body fluid balance, and improve blood circulation.

11. Rotation

Definition: A form of massage involving rotating the joint with one's own hands.

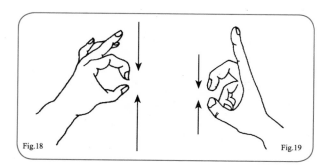

Fig.18   Fig.19

Action: Sitting down, take hold of the appropriate body part and rotate it with light and stable strength, building up gradually from light to heavy. The speed starts slow but quickens, gradually increasing the movement range of the joint, but always remaining within a physically acceptable range. Do not make violent movements. People with severe osteoarthritis and other diseases should take special care.

Common categories: Ankle rotation (Fig.20).

Functions: TCM believes that rotation can unblock meridian channels, promote the flow of *qi* and blood, improve joint movement and body condition. In the view of modern medicine, rotation can separate adhesion, alleviate spasm, restore joint movement, correct dislocation, improve circulation and tissue nutrition.

12. Wiping

Definition: A form of massage involving a wiping movement on acupoints (or parts) with the hands (or fingers).

Action: Press hands (or fingers) against the skin, using wrist

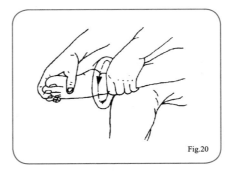

Fig.20

strength and combined breathing, make wiping actions up-and-down, side-to-side, or in a curving motion. The strength should be heavier than in the pushing method, but should progress from light to heavy to light. The strength should be even and gentle. To avoid damaging the skin, do not move too violently. The practitioner should feel a distinct mild ache initially, before a comfortable and refreshed feeling begins.

Common categories: Palm wiping, finger wiping, single-hand wiping, double-hand wiping (Fig.21).

Functions: TCM believes that wiping can harmonize *yin* and *yang*, unblock meridian and collateral channels, treat loss of consciousness, calm and refresh the brain, and reduce wrinkles. Modern medical research shows that wiping can expand blood vessels, improve metabolism, adjust the nervous system and body fluid circulation.

The above 12 methods mentioned are the basic techniques of massage, but in practice it is common to combine different techniques. The key technique is put first for purposes of emphasis, and is followed by the secondary one. For example, the "kneading-

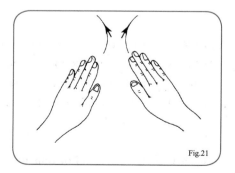

Fig.21

and-pressing technique" emphasizes kneading, where the strength is lighter; conversely, the "pressing-and-kneading technique" emphasizes pressing, where the strength is heavier.

1.7 Location of Acupoints

There are three ways of establishing acupoint location:

Body Indicators
Fixed indicators: the five sense organs, hair, hands and nails, nipples, navel, various bone and muscle indicators. For example, the center of the nipple is the Ruzhong point, the center of the navel is the Shenque point.

Non-fixed indicators: Acupoints that can be located by skin creases at joints, or by means of certain movements. For example, to locate the Lieque point, cross hands between the thumb and the index finger. The end of the index finger of one hand pinpoints the Lieque point above the wrist on the other. If you stand upright, with the hands pointing down naturally, the Fengshi point is located at the middle finger tip position.

Finger-length Measurement
Vertical *cun* measurement: The *cun* measurement is usually defined as the length of the second joint of the middle finger (Fig.22). Some people define one *cun* as the length of the last joint of the index finger, the addition of the middle joint producing two *cun*. The latter method is less often used.

Horizontal *cun* measurement: the width of four fingertips is three

34

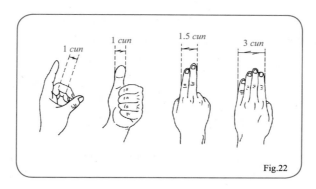

Fig.22

cun, and of two fingertip 1.5 *cun*. The width of the last thumb joint is one *cun* (Fig.22).

Bone Length Measurement
In order to locate meridian points far from body indicators, refer to Fig.23 in combination with the body indicator technique. Gender, age, weight and height are not relevant factors.

1.8 New Exercises for Preventing the Common Cold

These new exercises are helpful in preventing the common cold and also have a role in maintaining general health and youthfulness.

The common cold can lower the body's resistance and even lead to other diseases such as bronchitis, tracheitis and pneumonia. It is with reason that some people consider the common cold to be the source of many diseases.

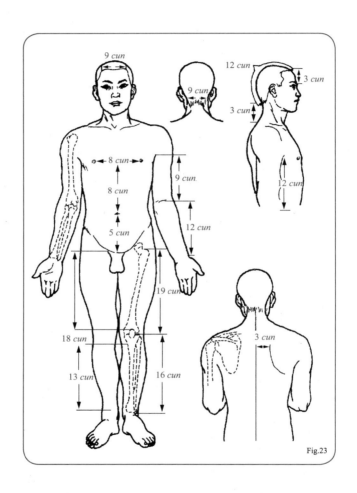

Fig.23

The exercises incorporate the effective elements from existing Chinese exercises and the records of some related documents. Based on these plus my personal experience, I have added two acupoints (Quchi and Zusanli), which also have the function of strengthening the constitution when fist knocking is applied.

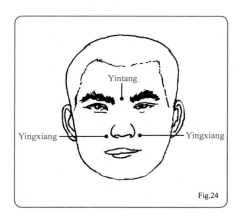

Fig.24

Fig.25

Exercise One

Lace the fingers of the hands and then rub the thumbs from the Yintang point (the midpoint between the eyebrows, Fig.24) to the Yingxiang points (in the nasolabial fold 0.5 *cun* lateral to the alanasi, Fig.24) 32 times. Using the edge and ball of the thumbs, rub the two wings of the nose 64 times (Fig.25).

Exercise Two

Knead-and-press the left Hegu acupoint with the right thumb, clockwise and counterclockwise each 32 times (Fig.27). Then change to the right Hegu point, repeating the actions with the same number of times. The Hegu (Fig.26) is located between the first and second metacarpal bones. It is the highest point formed when the thumb is resting against the index finger. Or the point can be found at the middle of the V formed by the metacarpal bones of the thumb and index finger (by placing the top phalanx of the other thumb in from the web when the thumb is extended).

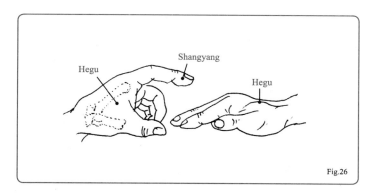

Fig.26

Fig.27

Exercise Three

Rub the palms up and down 32 times (Fig.28) then wipe the face with warm palms from forehead to chin (Fig.29); then divide the hands, moving along the cheeks to the ears, and then gently pull the ears up with the thumbs and index fingers 64 times (Fig.30).

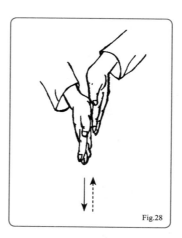

Fig.28

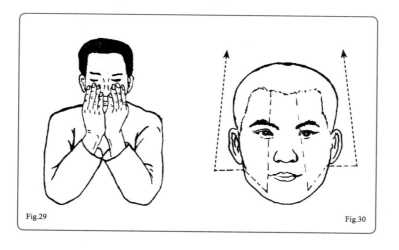

Fig.29

Fig.30

Exercise Four

Knead-and-press the Yingxiang points with the two index fingers, clockwise and counterclockwise, 32 times in each direction (Fig.31).

Exercise Five

Knock the left Quchi point (in the depression at the lateral end of elbow crease when the elbow is flexed) with the right fist 32 times (Fig.32). Change to the left fist, and knock the right Quchi 32 times (Fig.33).

Fig.31

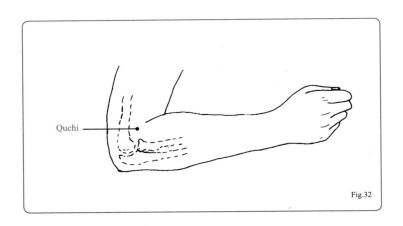

Quchi

Fig.32

Fig.33

42

Exercise Six

Rhythmically knock the left Zusanli point (three *cun* down from the middle of the kneecap and one finger's breadth lateral to the tibial crest, Fig.34), using the right fist (Fig.35), 32 times. Switch to the left fist to knock the right Zusanli.

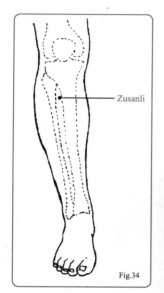

Zusanli

Fig.34

Fig.35

43

Notes:

- Wash your hands in warm water before starting.
- When doing the rubbing exercise, use the right degree of force. The acupoint should feel warm.
- Practice persistently and daily, morning or evening, doing six minutes each time.
- Wash your face and hands with cold water at least twice daily, morning and evening. This practice is very helpful for preventing the common cold.
- Keeping your toothbrush and tooth mug clean, and disinfecting them in a sterilizing cabinet are helpful in preventing the common cold.

1.9 New Exercises for the Nose

The respiratory system consists of the nose, pharynx, larynx, trachea, bronchia and bronchial organs in the lungs, and the lungs, which include alveoli, blood vessels, lymphatic vessels and nerves. Besides, there are also some assistant respiratory "devices," like pleura and so on. For improving the immune system, the microcirculation of nose, pharynx, larynx, trachea, bronchia and lung and the health level of the respiratory tract, I present some practical and convenient exercises for preventing common cold.

It goes without saying that breathing is very important for life. The nose, functioning as the gate for breathing, serves not only as the outlet of the lung but also has a close relationship with the internal organs, skin, muscles and joints (Fig.36).

44

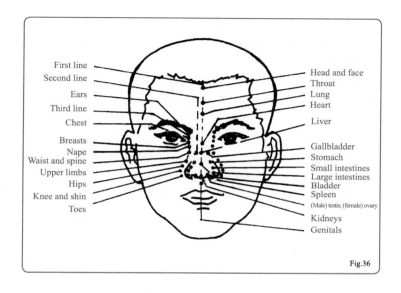

First line	Head and face
Second line	Throat
Ears	Lung
Third line	Heart
Chest	Liver
Breasts	
Nape	Gallbladder
Waist and spine	Stomach
Upper limbs	Small intestines
Hips	Large intestines
Knee and shin	Bladder
Toes	Spleen
	(Male) testis; (female) ovary
	Kidneys
	Genitals

Fig.36

Exercise One

1. With the flat tip of the index finger, press the Suliao (in the middle of the nose tip, Fig.37). Gently press it while inhaling and let go while exhaling. Repeat five to seven times.

2. Rhythmically tap with an index fingertip on the Suliao and repeat 32 times.

3. Knead the Suliao with an index finger, clockwise and counterclockwise, each eight times.

This step has the functions of invigorating *yang*, strengthening the kidneys, and relieving nasal blockage. It also has esthetic benefits.

Exercise Two

1. Place two index fingers on the two Yingxiang acupoints (in the nasolabial groove, at the level of the midpoint of the lateral border of the wings of the nose, Fig.37). Draw a full breath and press on the Yingxiang, and relax while exhaling (Fig.38). Repeat five to seven times.

2. Rhythmically tap the two Yingxiang acupoints with the two index fingertips. Repeat 32 times.

3. Knead the two Yingxiang with the two index fingertips, clockwise and counterclockwise, each eight times.

This step can relieve nasal blockage, dispel pathogenic wind-heat, and strengthen the body. It also has esthetic benefits.

Exercise Three

1. Put thumbs and index fingertips on the two Upper Yingxiang acupoints (0.5 *cun* below the eye inner canthus, (Fig.37). Press while inhaling and relax while exhaling. Repeat five to seven times.

2. Rhythmically tap the two upper Yingxiang with the two index fingertips. Repeat 32 times.

3. Knead the two upper Yingxiang with the two index fingers, clockwise and counterclockwise, eight times in each direction.

This step is effective in treating rhinitis It also has esthetic benefits, eliminating wrinkles.

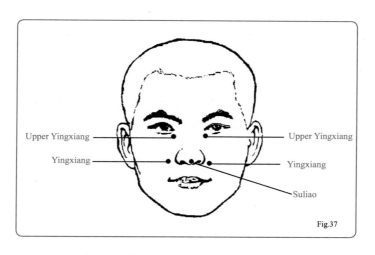

Upper Yingxiang ———— ———— Upper Yingxiang

Yingxiang ———— ———— Yingxiang

Suliao

Fig.37

Fig.38

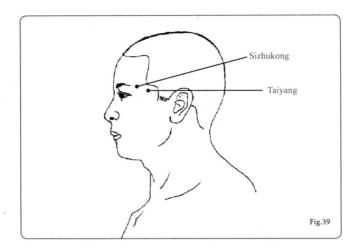

Sizhukong

Taiyang

Fig.39

Exercise Four

1. Put two thumbs on the two Taiyang acupoints (in the depression about one *cun* posterior to the midpoint between the lateral end of the eyebrows and the outer canthus, Fig.39). Press while inhaling and relax while exhaling. Repeat five to seven times.

2. Rhythmically tap the two Taiyang with the middle fingertips. Repeat 32 times.

3. Place the two middle fingertips flat on the forehead, then wipe-and-push via the two Taiyang towards the back of the head. Repeat 16 times.

This step has esthetic benefits, getting rid of winkles around the eyes. It also dispels wind and reduces fever.

Exercise Five

1. Press the Sizhukong acupoints (in the depression at the lateral end of the eyebrows, Fig.39) with the index fingertips and press the Yangbai acupoints (one *cun* directly above the midpoint of the eyebrows, Fig.40) with the middle fingertips. Press while inhaling and relax while exhaling. Repeat five to seven times.

2. Rhythmically tap the Sizhukong and Yangbai with the index and middle fingertips. Repeat 32 times.

3. Place the fingertips of the two hands flat on the forehead, then wipe-and-push via the two Yangbai and Sizhukong to the back of the head. Repeat 16 times.

This step has the functions of dispelling wind, clearing eyes, and reducing fever. It also gets rid of winkles.

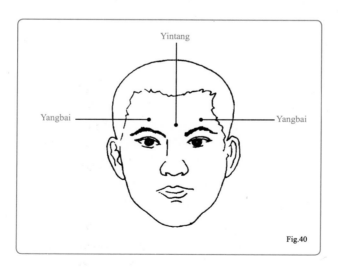

Fig.40

Exercise Six

1. Put the tips of the thumb and index finger of one hand on the lower edge of the septum nasi and lightly rub it eight times.

2. Using the middle fingertip of one hand, rhythmically knock the lower edge of the septum nasi in an upward direction 16 times.

3. Hold the lower edge of the septum nasi between the tips of the thumb and the index finger. Lightly pull it downward while inhaling and relax while exhaling (Fig.41). Repeat 16 times.

This step is effective for relieving nasal blockage, strengthening the waist and kidney. It also has esthetic benefits.

Exercise Seven

1. Insert the two index fingertips into the two nostrils. With the help of the index fingertips, softly rub the lower edges of the two nose wings with the two thumb tips. Repeat eight times.

2. Lightly tap the lower part of the two nose wings with the middle fingertips 16 times.

3. Insert the two index fingertips into the two nostrils. Lightly pull the lower edges of the two nose wings downward with the help of the two thumb tips (Fig.42). Repeat 16 times.

This step has the functions of relieving nasal blockage, benefiting the bladder, strengthening the limbs. It also lightens wrinkles.

Fig.41

Fig.42

Exercise Eight

1. Put the two middle fingertips on the inner canthus of the eyes and softly rub along both sides of the nose bridge, downwards and upwards five to seven times (Fig.43).

2. Make two fists with the thumb covering the thumb side of the fist (Fig.44). Lightly tap the sides of the nose bridge with the back of the thumb joint first downwards and then upwards (Fig.45), eight knocks up and eight knocks down.

3. Place the tips of the thumb and the index finger of one hand on the inner canthus of each eye, and softly wipe and pull downward along both sides of the nose bridge while inhaling; stop doing it while exhaling (Fig.46). Do the same movements with the other hand. Repeat eight times.

This step has the effects of helping *qi* circulation, and strengthening the body. It also lightens wrinkles.

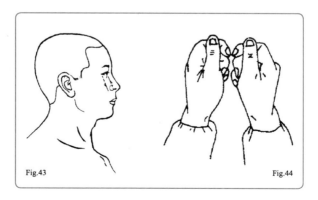

Fig.43   Fig.44

Fig.45

Fig.46

Exercise Nine

1. Put a middle fingertip on the Yintang (in the middle of the two eyebrows, Fig.40). Press down while inhaling and release while exhaling. Repeat five to seven times.

2. Stop the left nostril by pressing the left index fingertip against the left side of the nose. Then make a fist with the right hand and gently rub the right wing of the nose with the front of the right thumb, upwards and downwards eight times (Figs.47, 48). (Draw a full breath before rubbing, and exhale through the right nostril while rubbing). Switch hands and rub the left wing of the nose in the same way. Repeat three times.

Fig.48

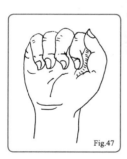

Fig.47

Fig.49

54

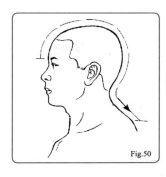

Fig.50

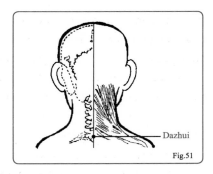

Dazhui

Fig.51

3. Rub the two hands warm. Wipe-and-push with the two middle fingers, putting one in front of the other (Fig.49), from the Yintang over the forehead, crown and occiput (Fig.50), and ending at the Dazhui (below the spinous process of the seventh cervical vertebra (Fig.51). Repeat 16 times.

This step has the functions of dispelling wind, calming the mind and beautifying.

Those who suffer from allergic rhinitis, atrophic rhinitis, nasosinusitis, blocked nose, running nose, or poor sense of smell should avoid catching cold in the nose. Do nose and head massage daily for three minutes whilst taking a warm shower. For even better effects, do this exercise together with Exercise Five, Exercise Six, Exercise Seven and Exercise Eight.

1.10 New Exercises for the Mouth

The exercises in this section are helpful for preventing and treating flu. Furthermore, they have the functions of preventing and curing dental diseases, periodontal diseases, strengthening the body, beautifying, and extending the lifespan.

According to TCM theory, the spleen opens into the mouth and is manifest on the lips. The kidney is in charge of bones, and the teeth are an extension of the bones. The tongue is the mirror of the heart. Therefore, the protection and health of the lips, teeth and tongue are very important for the human body.

Studies indicate: saliva consists of various kinds of enzymes which can not only protect the gastric wall, repair the gastric mucosa, invigorate digestion and resist aging, but also play an anticancer role. For instance, saliva consists of such substances as oxidase and peroxidase, which are able to eliminate such carcinogenic substances as aflatoxin, 3,4-benzopyrene and nitrite. In addition, saliva also contains hormones, vitamins, inorganic salts, proteins, etc. It has the functions of preventing and curing dental diseases, improving the constitution, beautifying and prolonging life.

Huangting Neijing Jing, a classic on health cultivation through the internal-power arts, records that saliva has the function of "smoothing the meridian channels and promote blood circulation, making the face radiant with health, consolidating teeth and keeping hair black."

Exercise One
1. Place the index finger of one hand on the Renzhong acupoint

(a little above the philtrum midpoint, Fig.52) and the thumb on the Chengjiang acupoint (in the depression in the center of the mentolabial groove, Fig.52): Inhale while pressing and exhale while relaxing (Fig.53). Repeat five to seven times.

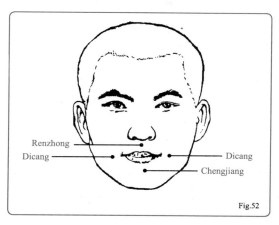

Fig.52

Fig.53

2. Rhythmically and lightly, tap the Renzhong and Chengjiang with the tips of the two middle fingertips, each 16 times.

3. Using the thumb side of the index fingers, rub the Renzhong and Chengjiang in a crosswise direction (Fig.54), each 16 times.

This exercise has the functions of improving local metabolism, calming restlessness, benefiting the lumbar vertebra, treating deviation of eyes and mouth. It also beautifies the lips and delays the greying of the beard.

Exercise Two

1. Place the flat aspect of each index finger on each Dicang acupoint (0.4 *cun* lateral to the corner of the mouth, Fig.52). Inhale when pressing and exhale when relaxing (Fig.55). Repeat five to seven times.

2. Rhythmically tap the two Dicang with the two index fingertips simultaneously, 16 times each.

3. Using the thumb side of the index fingers, rub both Dicang acupoints in a vertical direction (Fig.56) simultaneously, 16 times each.

This exercise is effective in preventing and curing facial paralysis. It also beautifies the lips and darkens the beard.

Fig.54

Fig.55

Fig.56

Exercice Three

1. Place the flat aspect of the thumbs on the Xiaguan acupoints at each side of the face (in the depression between the mandibular notch and the inferior border of the zygomatic arch, Fig.57). Press when inhaling and relax when exhaling (Fig.58). Repeat five to seven times.

2. Using the two middle fingertips, rhythmically tap the two Xiaguan simultaneously, 16 times each.

3. Rub the palms together until warm and then rub the two Xiaguan upwards and downwards 32 times.

This exercise is effective in promoting blood circulation, diminish inflammation, relieving pain. It also has esthetic benefits.

Exercice Four

Apply the same actions and sequence as in Exercise Three to the two Jiache acupoints (one finger-breadth anterior and superior

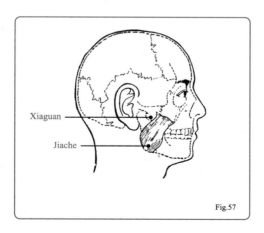

Fig.57

60

Fig.58

to the lower angle of the jaw at the prominence of the masseter muscle when the teeth are clenched, Fig.57).

This exercise has the functions of dispersing harmful wind, smoothing blood, benefiting the teeth. It decreases wrinkles and beautifies the lips.

Exercise Five

1. Stretch out the tongue and exhale for a few seconds (Fig.59), withdraw and inhale. Repeat five to seven times.

Fig.59

2. Open the mouth wide and exhale for a few seconds. Inhale as you close. Then lightly gnash the teeth, and clench them for a few seconds. Repeat five to seven times.

3. Move the tip of the tongue over the upper and lower gums inside and outside the teeth. Do this eight times in clockwise and counterclockwise directions. Then flush with the resulting saliva 16 times (Fig.60), and gently swallow the saliva in three mouthfuls, focusing concentration on the Qihai acupoint (1.5 *cun* below the navel, Fig.61).

Having finished this three-step exercise, repeat it three times.

These movements are good for strengthening teeth, spleen and stomach and for preventing gum atrophy. They make for beautiful lips and fewer wrinkles.

Exercise Six
Gently chew the upper lip with the lower teeth 16 times (Fig.62). Then repeat with the upper teeth on the lower lip (Fig.63).

These movements improve assimilation. They also beautify the lips and darken the beard.

Fig.60

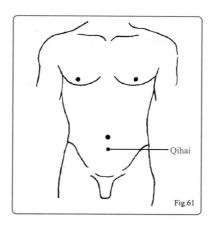

Qihai

Fig.61

Fig.62

Fig.63

Exercise Seven

Rub the palms warm, and then wipe-and-push with the fingers from the medial point of the lower jaw up to the anterior hairline and then move along the sides of the head to the occiput (Fig.64). Repeat 16 times.

This step is effective for clearing the brain, and regulating the meridians. Esthetic benefits include fewer wrinkles, moister lips and darker beard.

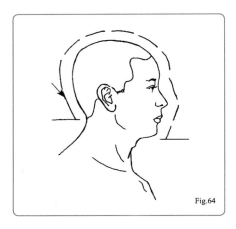

Fig.64

Notes:

● Method of Reinforcing Teeth and Kidney Essence: Close mouth and clench teeth tightly when having a bowel movement or passing water. Since, in TCM, the kidney is in charge of the bones, and teeth are an extension of the bones, this method can help strengthen the kidney by preventing kidney *qi* dissipation. Hence it has the above-mentioned functions.

● Face-beautifying, Anti-aging and Anti-cancer Method: There is research indicating that 70-90% of cancer cases are caused by carcinogenic substances in the external environment. One American scientific survey reports that one-third of all cases of cancer in men and one half of all in women are related to improper food and drink. Therefore, some Japanese scholars, in view of saliva playing a defensive role against cancer, have spread the "30-mouthfuls movement," advocating that all food (including juicy food) should be chewed 30 times, believing this way of eating really can prevent cancer. There are some scientific grounds for this belief.

• In the context of Chinese food habits, chewing each mouthful 30 times could be difficult to sustain. However, we should try to chew more when eating. If one can stick to this habit it will be beneficial in preventing cancer, beautifying the face, slimming and resisting ageing.

1.11 New Exercises for the Neck

The content of this section is helpful in preventing and treating the common cold and also has a role in maintaining general health and youthfulness.

Medical researches indicate the benefit of neck exercises in maintaining a youthful appearance. This is because wrinkles usually appear on the neck earlier than on the face. The neck is the head's only passage in *qi* and blood circulation to the internal organs, the four limbs and to the bones of the body. Close observation will show that a person with a good constitution generally has a strong neck and a frail person usually has a weak neck. Therefore, it is very important to learn the methods of keeping the neck beautiful and healthy.

Exercise One

1. Press the Qiaogong (a line between the Yifeng and Quepen. The Yifeng is located behind the earlobe in the depression between the mandible and mastoid process. The Quepen is located in the center of the supraclavicular fossa, directly above the nipple, Fig.65). Put the right middle fingertip on the left Yifeng and gently press while inhaling and relax while exhaling. Keep pressing and move in a downward direction along the Qiaogong line to the Quepen. Change to the left hand and use the middle finger tip on the right Qiaogong. Repeat five to seven times.

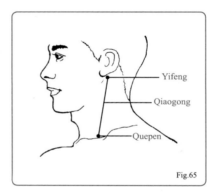

Fig.65

2. Using the four fingers (not the thumb) of the right hand, rhythmically and lightly tap the left Qiaogong. Switch to the left hand and do the same on the right Qiaogong line. This sequence is considered as one operation. Repeat eight times.

3. Straighten the fingers of the right hand and close them naturally. Place them on the left side of the neck with the middle fingertip on the left Yifeng. Wipe with the right hand via the Qiaogong line downward to the left Quepen. Repeat 16 times. Switch to the left hand and wipe the right Qiaogong line 16 times.

66

This exercise is very effective for improving hearing and eyesight, dispersing wind, regulating the meridians, stopping hiccups, and lowering high blood pressure. It also gets rid of neck wrinkles.

Exercise Two

1. Straighten the four fingers (not the thumb) of the right hand and close them naturally. Place them on the left side thyroid gland (on the lower part of the throat and the upper sides of the windpipe, Fig.66). Press down while inhaling and relax while exhaling. Repeat five to seven times. Switch to the left hand and perform the same action to the left side of the thyroid five to seven times.

2. Lightly tap the left side of the thyroid with the four fingers of the right hand 16 times. Switch to the left hand and perform the same action on the right side of the thyroid 16 times.

Fig.66

3. Rub the hands warm (Fig.67) and then rub with the four fingers of the right hand on the left side of the thyroid, up and down 16 times. Rub the hands warm again and repeat the same action 16 times on the right side of the thyroid, using the left hand.

These steps are generally beneficial to health, hair and skin.

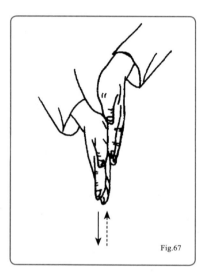

Fig.67

Exercise Three

1. Place the right middle fingertip on the Tiantu acupoint (in the center of the suprasternal fossa, Fig.68) and press (moving downward along the thoracic bone) while inhaling, releasing while exhaling, Fig.69). Repeat five to seven times.

2. Lightly and rhythmically tap the Tiantu with the middle fingertip of the right hand 16 times.

3. Knead the Tiantu with the middle fingertip of the right hand clockwise and counterclockwise, eight times in each direction.

This step has the functions of relieving cough and regulating the throat condition.

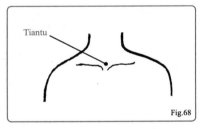

Tiantu

Fig.68

Fig.69

69

Exercise Four

1. Stand straight (Fig.70). While exhaling, bow the head as low as possible till it touches the chest (Fig.71), and inhale as you return to the original position. On the next exhalation lean the head back (Fig.72), and inhale as you return to the original position. Repeat 16 times.

Fig.70

Fig.71

Fig.72

2. Lean the head leftward while exhaling (Fig.73), return while inhaling. Lean the head rightward (Fig.74) while exhaling, return while inhaling. Repeat 16 times.

Fig.73   Fig.74

3. Turn the head leftward while exhaling (Fig.75), return while inhaling. Turn the head rightward while exhaling (Fig.76), return while inhaling. Repeat 16 times.

Fig.75

Fig.76

73

4. Rotate the head, first clockwise (Fig.77), and then counter-clockwise (Fig.78). Repeat eight times in each direction.

5. Rub the palms warm and place one on each side of the back neck (Fig.79), then rub lelft and right simultaneously. Repeat 16 times. Rub the palms warm again and then wipe-and-push over the neck, the face, up to the crown, and then down to the nape (Fig.80). Repeat 16 times.

These steps are very effective for strengthening the neck, and getting rid of aches and pains in the head, shoulders and upper back. They also have anti-aging and esthetic benefits.

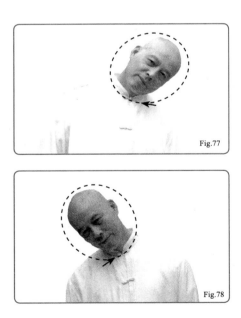

Fig.77

Fig.78

Fig.79

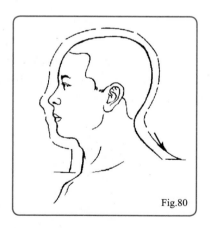

Fig.80

Exercise Five

1. Lie on the back with the arms at the sides of the body (Fig.81). While exhaling, slowly raise the legs (Fig.82) and then the trunk until they are perpendicular to the ground. Support the back with the hands and tuck the chin into the chest (Fig.83). Maintain the posture as long as possible (beginners may do it for a short time only), then gently revert to the original position (for the sake of the heart, do not stand up abruptly). Repeat three times.

2. After finishing Step 1, straighten the hands and place them on the either side of the body using only the shoulders, neck and the back of the head to support the body (Fig.84). Other movements are as in Step 1.

These steps have the effect of calming the mind, helping sleep, and preventing and curing neck and shoulder pains. They also have esthetic benefits.

Notes:

● People with high blood pressure and neck vertebra problems should not force themselves to do Exercise Five if they feel it sinappropriate for their particular condition.

Fig.81

Fig.82

Fig.83

Fig.84

● Lead a regular life, and never eat and drink too much. Cultivate good health habits — getting up and going to bed early, eating plenty of fresh vegetables, fruit and other nutritious food.

● Being honest and tolerant with an optimistic attitude and broad mind is helpful to staying young and living longer. The secret of long life is a positive attitude.

● The saying "Life exists in movement" underlines the importance of movement in our lives. We should take exercise in line with our preferences — for example, Taijiquan shadow boxing, health exercises, *qigong*, yoga, swimming, jogging and relaxing the body while listening to light music.

● Here are some suggestions for those suffering chronic laryngeal irritation and cough: ①Hold and melt pear or loquat syrup in the mouth with the dosage prescribed on the instructions. ②Rub the afflicted parts and neck for two to three minutes with a board (jade or oxhorn) for the *guasha* treatment, once in the morning and once in the evening. Rub the skin reddish but do not break it. Before rubbing, you may daub essential balm or massage cream on afflicted parts and neck in order to decrease the friction and increase the healing effect. Sustaining this practice for a long term can bring good results. ③Massage afflicted parts and neck with an electric massager for 10 minutes, twice daily. Sustained long-term practice is helpful to root out the symptom (this method is unsuitable for those with hemorrhagic tendency or with blood in the saliva).

● Those with severe throat pain (including third-degree acute suppurative swelling of tonsils) could try pricking a three-edge needle or entry needle into the Shaoshang acupoint (0.1 *cun* lateral to the thumb nail, Fig.85) until a little blood appears of its own accord or at a light squeeze. Usually, the throat pain will be relieved immediately. If the afflicted part is in the left side of the neck, prick the left Shaoshang; if on the right side of the neck, the right Shaoshang; if on both sides, the two Shaoshang. Do this once a day or every other day. Before taking this step, sterilization of the needle and of the acupoint is necessary: ①Sterilize the needle in a sterilizer or soak it for 30 minutes in rubbing alcohol (75%). ②The Shaoshang acupoint should be cleaned twice with rubbing alcohol (75%). ③The person inserting the needle should wear sterilized medical rubber finger covers or gloves. The methods described in the last two points can be used separately, but using them in combination will produce better effects. In a clinical situation, they can be implemented along with other treatments, for eliminating toxins and increasing efficacy.

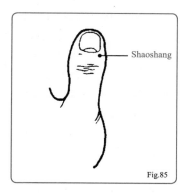

Fig.85

1.12 How to Strengthen the Chest and Defend Against Cancer

The content of this section can help us comfortably improve the microcirculation and functions of heart and lungs by means of self-massage on the chest. These methods not only help against flu: they are also able to reinforce the functions of heart and lungs and promote the flow of *qi* so as to ease difficult and labored breathing, benefit the pharynx, smooth out throat, nourish the liver, relieve pain and dysphoria, thus strengthening the constitution and helping to ward off cancer. This is because they help maintain and promote the secretion of thymosin, a protein that promotes the development of immune-system cells, thus helpful in increasing the resistance to cancer and other diseases.

Exercise One

1. Place one thumb tip on the Danzhong (on the level of the fourth intercostal space, at the midpoint of the line between the nipples, Fig.86) and press down. Press the Danzhong while inhaling and lift while exhaling (Fig.87). Repeat five to seven times.

2. Form a fist naturally and then knock the Danzhong rhythmically with the closed face of the fist (Fig.88). With clenched teeth and closed mouth, exhale with a snort through the nose, relaxing on inhalation. Repeat 16 times.

3. Knead the Danzhong with the flat tip of one thumb clockwise and counterclockwise, eight times in each direction.

This exercise is effective in regulating the flow of *qi*, eliminating stuffiness from the chest and easing anxiety, etc.

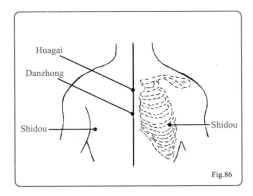

Fig.86

Exercise Two

Press the Huagai acupoint (on the anterior midline, on the level of the first intercostal space, Fig.86) and perform actions 1-3 of Exercise One, in the same order.

This exercise has the effect expelling staleness and taking in freshness, strengthening lung function and improving respiration.

Exercise Three

1. Put the right middle fingertip on the left Shidou (in the fifth intercostal space, six *cun* lateral to the anterior midline, Fig.86). Softly press down on the Shidou while inhaling (softly, slowly and lightly, without force), and lift while exhaling. Repeat five to seven times. Switch to the left middle finger and do likewise on the right Shidou. Repeat five to seven times.

2. Lightly tap the left Shidou rhythmically with the right palm 16 times. Change to the left palm and tap the right Shidou 16 times.

3. Knead the left Shidou with the flat of the right middle fingertip, clockwise and counterclockwise, eight times in each direction. Switch to the left middle fingertip and do the same to the right Shidou.

This exercise can get rid of the distended pain in the chest and hypochondrium and improve spleen function.

Exercise Four

1. Place the flat of each thumb on each Zhangmen acupoint (on the lateral sides of the abdomen, below the free end of the 11th rib; or at the point level with your elbow when you bend your arm against your side, Fig.89). Press down while inhaling and relax while exhaling. Repeat five to seven times.

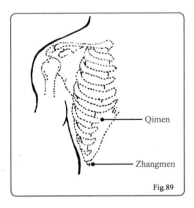

Fig.89

2. With the base of both palms, softly and rhythmically knock the two Zhangmen 16 times.

3. Using the flat of each thumb, knead the two Zhangmen clockwise and counterclockwise, eight times in each direction.

82

Fig.90

This exercise is effective in removing stagnation of the liver, replenishing the spleen and relieving digestive pains, and preventing and treating darkened forehead.

Exercise Five

1. Rub the palms warm (Fig.90) and wipe-and-push the palms downward 32 times over the thymus gland (behind the broad, upper part of the sternum).

2. Make a natural fist and with the closed face of the fist lightly tap the chest above the thymus, working in a downward direction while exhaling with a snort through the nose; rest while inhaling. Repeat the sequence eight times.

3. Do Step 1 of this exercise again 32 times.

This exercise is effective for relieving dysphoria and stuffiness of the chest, resisting cancer, prolonging lifespan and promoting heart and lung functions.

Exercise Six

1. Rest the left hand on the top of the head. With the second segments of the four fingers of the right hand, knead-and-press the left chest along the intercostal spaces of the true ribs, working downwards and outwards, until a sensation of mild pain and distension is felt (Fig.91). Carry out the same action five to seven times on the right chest, using the left hand (Fig.92). The sequence is considered as one time. Repeat five to seven times.

Fig.91

Fig.92

2. Grasp the left thorax muscle with the right hand while exhaling, relax while inhaling (Fig.93). Repeat five to seven times. Switch to the left hand and repeat five to seven times to the right thorax muscle.

3. Put the left hand on the top of the head and the right palm rubs the left chest ribs, working downwards and outwards following the intercostal spaces between the true ribs (Fig.94). Repeat five to seven times. Switch to the left palm and carry out the same procedure on the right side, also five to seven times.

4. With the left hand on top of the head, and using the right palm, tap the left chest ribs, working downwards (Fig.95). Tapping the

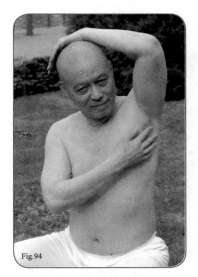
Fig.94

right chest ribs in the same manner, using the left palm (Fig.96). Repeat five to seven times each side.

5. With the left hand on top of the head, use the right palm to rub the left chest ribs downwards, 16 times. Change the left palm and do the same the right chest rib (Fig.97).

These exercises can improve heart and lung function, benefit the pharynx and ease difficult and labored breathing; they have a role in relieving pain and discomfort, resisting cancer and preventing skin aging.

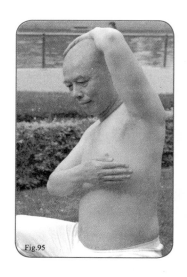

Fig.95

Fig.96

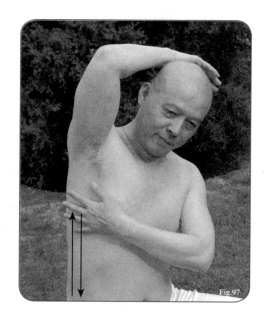

Fig.97

86

1.13 New Self-Massage for Improving Immunity

As well as helping ward off and cure the common cold, the exercises of this section are also useful against chronic bronchitis, strengthening the body and improving immunity.

Adopt any position, like lying, sitting or standing (according to your physical situation) to do the following exercises seriously and patiently.

1. Nose

Knead the Yingxiang acupoint (in the nasolabial fold 0.5 *cun* lateral to the alanasi, Fig.98), with the flat of the index fingertips for one minute (Fig.99).

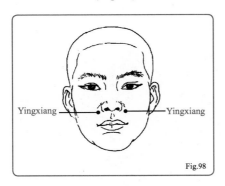

Fig.98

Fig.99

From the left side of the nose and using the flat of the left index fingertip, stop the left nostril. Then make a fist with the right hand and gently rub the right wing of the nose with the front side of the thumb, up and down eight times. (Draw a full breath before rubbing and exhale through the right nostril while rubbing, Fig.100). Switch hands and rub the left nose wing in the same way (These steps are considered as one time). Repeat three times.

Put the flat of the thumb and the index finger of one hand on the inner canthus of the two eyes (each side of the nose bridge) and press and pull downwards. Exhale through the nostrils while using strength, and rest while inhaling. Switch to the other hand and do the same. Keep doing this for one minute (Fig.101).

Fig.100

Fig.101

2. Head and Neck

Place the middle fingertip on the Tiantu (in the center of the suprasternal fossa, Fig.102) and knead for one minute (Fig.103).

Rub the palms warm (Fig.104). Push in an upwards direction from the Tiantu to the neck, face and crown. Then push downwards from the occipital bone to behind the ears, the two sides of the neck, and the Tiantu. Repeat for one minute.

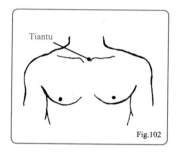

Fig.102

Fig.103

Fig.104

3. Abdomen

Using the flat of the thumb tip, knead-and-press the Zhongwan acupoint (in the median line, four *cun* above the navel, Figs. 125,105), the Shenque acupoint (in the center of the navel, Figs.125, 106) and the Guanyuan acupoint (in the median line, three *cun* below the navel, Fig.125). Repeat for one minute.

Rub the palms warm and push from the xiphoid down to the pubis. Then, divide the hands and push along the two groin areas and the two sides of the abdomen, returning to the lower edge of the xiphoid (Fig.107). Repeat for one minute.

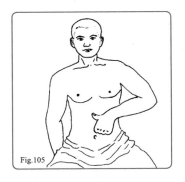
Fig.105

Fig.106

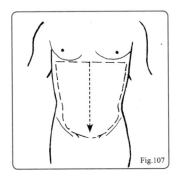
Fig.107

4. Waist

Clench the hands into fists and put them behind the body. Using the index finger knuckles, knead-and-press the two Shenyu acupoints (1.5 *cun* lateral to the lower edge of the lumbar vertebra, Fig.124) for one minute.

Rub the palms warm and rub the waist up-and-down and side to side for one minute (Figs.108, 109).

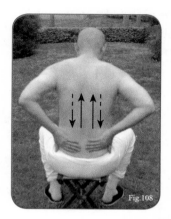

Fig.108

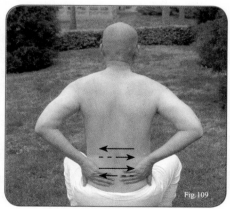

Fig.109

5. Upper Limbs

Using the ulnar side of the right fist, rhythmically knock the left Quchi point (in the depression at the lateral end of the crease when the arm is flexed, Fig.110), 32 times (Fig.111). Then switch to the left fist to knock the right Quchi 32 times. The right degree of strength produces a slight soreness.

Rub the palms warm, then massage the left arm with the right palm, working from the chest to fingertips along the inside of the arm (Fig.135), and then from fingertips to shoulder on the outside (Fig.134) for one minute. Repeat the complete procedure using the left hand on the right arm.

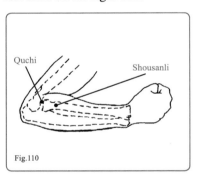

Fig.110

Fig.111

6. Lower Limbs

Using the ulnar sides of the fists knock the left and right Zusanli for one minute, the right fist knocking the left Zusanli (Fig.112).

Rub the palms warm and then using the right palm, rub warm the left Yongquan (on the sole of the foot, between the second and third metatarsal bones, approximately 1/3 the distance between the base of the second toe and the heel, in a depression formed when the foot is plantar flexed, Figs.113, 114). Rub the palms warm again and repeat the procedure with the other hand on the other foot. Doing this long-term, once in the morning and once in the evening, will produce the finest results.

Fig.112

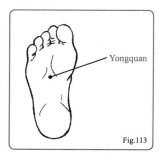

Yongquan

Fig.113

Fig.114

Chapter 2

NEW TCM ANTI-FLU THERAPY

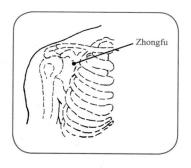

2.1 Treating the Root Cause and Symptoms with a Hair Drier

The inappropriate use of medication by people who have caught cold can often cause complications. According to an article in the *Yangtse Evening Post* of April 10, 1997, a college student in Tianjin caught a cold and took medicine indiscriminately, thus causing a drug rash reaction. Sadly, he ultimately died of kidney failure. Therefore, my suggestion is when you catch cold, no matter how light the condition is or how busy you are, take it seriously; go see a doctor before taking any medicine, and take it according to the doctor's instructions.

"Cold" can be divided into the common cold and influenza (flu), both of which are called upper respiratory tract infection (RTI) in medical terminology. "Cold" is a common ailment in humans, and is caused by a virus. Influenza can lead to acute upper respiratory tract infection, which is very common and harmful to health. "Cold" can be caught at any time of the year, mostly during autumn, winter and spring. According to medical research, every year there are between 600 million and 1.2 billion incidences of "colds" across the world. The global figure for deaths from influenza is between 250,000 and 500,000 people. People working in high-rises, particularly those in stressful occupations, are more vulnerable to infection.

1. The common cold is also known as acute coryza, upper respiratory tract catarrhal infection or a cold. It is primarily caused by rhinoviruses, human parainfluenza viruses, human respiratory syncytial virus, ECHO virus and coxsackie virus. TCM designates it as externally contracted disease, one caused by pathogenic wind

invading the lung. Its incubation period is 12-72 hours, during which the symptoms are relatively light. Early phase symptoms include mild chill, sore throat, sneezing, nasal congestion, runny nose and watery eyes. After one or two days, the symptoms gradually get heavier, mainly including breathing difficulty, cough, headache, tight chest, malaise, aching muscles and fatigue. Some may experience constipation or diarrhea, some loss of taste, mild fever and thin sputum. Otolaryngology examination might reveal congestion and dropsy of turbinate mucosa, runny nose and congestion of the throat, and tonsil congestion and hypertrophy. After three to five days, the nasal mucus becomes thick and yellow. After about a week, all the symptoms generally resolve.

2. The flu is an acute infection of the upper respiratory tract caused by influenza viruses (including influenza A virus, influenza B virus and influenza C virus). According to TCM, flu is "epidemic cold," "seasonal cold," "wind-warm" or "spring-warm" syndrome, and is caused by pestilence invading the lung. Flu attacks people rapidly in the early phase, and then spreads wide. The symptoms of flu are complicated, mainly including sudden chills, shivering, high fever, muscle pains, severe headache, reddening of the eyes and face, weakness and general discomfort. However, the respiratory tract symptoms are light or unnoticeable. The high fever generally lasts two to three days, with body temperatures reaching 39-40°C. Other symptoms are sneezing, nasal congestion, runny nose, thirst, sore throat, dry cough or cough with thin sputum. Influenza may produce nausea, vomiting and serious diarrhea, giving the disease another name — "gastric flu." In some patients, influenza may harm the cardiovascular and nervous systems, leading to obstinate fever, delirium, coma, or even dropping of blood pressure and shock, putting the life in serious danger.

3. A ten-year long, £6 million study by British scientists concluded that there is no ideal method or specific drug to cure flu. All medication can do is to relieve the symptoms. There is consensus among the international medical community that the best way to prevent flu is vaccination. Vaccination can reduce the incidence of flu; however, the many strains and high mutation rate of influenza viruses (influenza A virus in particular), make it very difficult to guard against completely.

Now, the prevailing principle in medical circles is to relieve the symptoms, conserve the body's energy, reduce the course of the disease and prevent complications. There are two opinions vis-a-vis people with cold: One is that it should be treated right away; the second view is that one should not jump to treatment in the early phase, since there is no specific drug and catching the infection helps mobilize the body's own resistance. According to medical research, the second one is correct. However, it is well known that flu attacks rapidly, spreads widely, and causes serious consequences — this makes it hard to implement the second view universally. Many medical workers and researchers are making unremitting efforts to solve the problem of cold, especially flu.

Is it possible for us to create a new method to cure flu? It is the wish of one and all to find a new, scientific, simple and effective cure, one that is safe and without side effects, one that can directly kill the flu virus, improve blood circulation, and build up resistance to disease, one with remarkable curative effect, that can accelerate recovery, an economic, non-pharmaceutical method of controlling or stopping the spread of flu....

4. Based on my clinical experience and research of over 30 years,

I introduce you a new method for treating colds and flu at the early stage. It tackles the problem of the variability of influenza viruses, and is in accordance with the scientific principles that high temperatures can directly kill all influenza viruses and improve microcirculation. It incorporates the results of research in ECIWO (Embryo Containing the Information of the Whole Organism) biology and TCM theory of meridians. Following the treatment the patient feels relaxed. In all cases use an electric hair dryer on a warm setting from a distance of 10 cm.

1) Direct the hot air upwards to the Suliao point (tip of the nose, Fig.115) and the two nostrils for five to eight minutes (Fig.116).

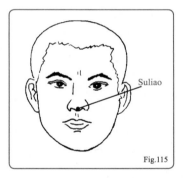

Fig.115

Fig.116

2) According to ECIWO biological research, the second metacarpal (Fig.117) has a physiological relationship with other parts of the human body (Fig.118).

Direct hot air onto the second metacarpal bone (Fig.119). Do each hand for three to five minutes.

3) Direct hot air onto the Dazhui point (below the spinous process of the seventh cervical vertebra, Fig.120) for 3-5 minutes (Fig.121).

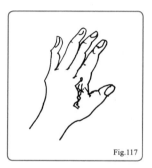

Fig.117

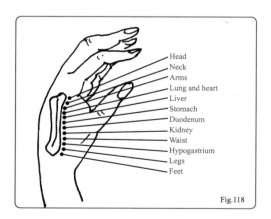

Head
Neck
Arms
Lung and heart
Liver
Stomach
Duodenum
Kidney
Waist
Hypogastrium
Legs
Feet

Fig.118

100

Fig.119

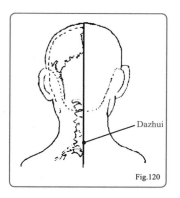

Dazhui

Fig.120

Fig.121

4) Direct hot air onto the Yongquan point (in the depression on the sole when the foot is in plantar flexion, approximately at the junction of the anterior and middle third of the sole [not counting toes], Fig.122). Do each foot for three to five minutes (Fig.123).

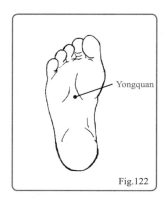

Yongquan

Fig.122

Fig.123

This method seizes the nucleus of the flu virus, which is protein. Protein is sensitive to and can be rendered inactive by high temperatures. According to scientific research, inhibition of the activity of flu virus begins when the temperature reaches 39°C. When it hits 40°C, inactivation of the virus starts, a process that accelerates as the temperature increases. Based on other research, it takes 30 minutes at 56°C to inactivate avian influenza flu virus, 10 minutes at 60°C, two minutes at 66°C, and two seconds at 70°C. The H1N1 virus will be inactivated at 72°C.

The following points have been arrived at on the basis of modern acupuncture and acupressure research, animal experiments, and clinical studies:

a. Suliao point: The improving of the microcirculation of the Suliao point is effective in regulating breathing rate and rhythm and abnormal breathing, and in treating respiratory failure. It is also effective in regulating the motion of gastric involuntary muscle. Directing hot air onto the Suliao will improve microcirculation in the Suliao and nose; alleviate symptoms — nasal congestion, runny nose and sneezing; directly inhibit and inactivate the flu virus; and control and stop its spread.

b. The second metacarpal bone: Improving microcirculation of the second metacarpal bone will improve lung ventilation; reduce obstruction in the respiratory tract; regulate the motion of involuntary muscle of bronchus and bronchiole; tighten and alleviate swelling in the bronchial mucosa, thus improving lung ventilation function and relieving asthma. It can also ease tension in the cerebral veins; enhance the elasticity of the arteries and increase the blood supply, thus improving the blood supply to the brain. It is also effective in regulating white blood cells, platelets, as well as the endocrine system including gonads, thyroid gland, pituitary-adrenal gland cortex and adrenal gland medulla, especially the central nervous system and the immunity of the whole body. Therefore, application of hot air to the second metacarpal bone will not only improve microcirculation of the second metacarpal bone and innate resistance to flu, but also mitigate symptoms, accelerate recovery, and improve appearance and health.

c. Dazhui point: The improving of the microcirculation of the Dazhui acupoint can enhance lung function and ventilation, alleviate bronchial spasm, and reduce obstruction in the respiratory tract. Not only can it rapidly reduce symptoms, it can produce obvious improvement in lung function, electrocardiogram and immunity. It can also influence the thermoregulatory center, "lowering the thermostat" and exciting the sweating system, thereby causing the sweat glands to sweat copiously, and dilating the blood vessels to the sweat glands and the skin. In this way, it helps bring down fever. Therefore, blowing the Dazhui with hot air is effective not only in improving the microcirculation of the Dazhui and alleviating flu symptoms including high fever; it also raises the immunity of the whole body and accelerates recovery.

d. Yongquan point: Improving Yongquan microcirculation has a beneficial effect on the distribution of white blood cells in peripheral blood circulation, helping to keep the normal amount of white blood cells. It has diuretic properties, helps reduce blood pressure, tones the kidneys and makes one sleep peacefully. According to my long-term observation and clinical experience with flu patients, the temperature at the Yongquan points and the skin of their toes is comparatively low. Directing hot air onto the Yongquan point for several minutes will dramatically raise the temperature of the Yongquan and bring about noticeable alleviation of the flu symptoms including nasal congestion, runny nose and fever. It can also make the patient sweat all over, giving him a relaxed feeling. This is probably because the action can influence the thermoregulatory center, "lower the thermostat" and excite the sweating system, thus making the sweat glands produce sweat, and dilating blood vessels to the sweat glands and the skin, thereby helping reduce fever. The other possibility is that it can improve the systems of heart, lung, immunity and nerves, and activate the system of endomorphines. The matter awaits further research. Some scholars have used meridian monitors to examine the Yongquan points of flu sufferers and found that they have a deficiency of *qi* in the kidney meridian of foot-Shaoyin (one of the 12 meridians, which begins on the plantar tip of the little toe and travels up to the head via Yongquan). Since "kidney is congenital essence" and the Yongquan is the source of foot-Shaoyin, hot air treatment of the Yongquan will improve its microcirculation, enhance the immunity of the whole body, relieve flu symptoms and accelerate recovery.

Notes:

These methods can be used by themselves or in coordination with other methods of treatment. It will enhance the prevention and treatment of flu, shorten its duration, avoid and reduce complications, and accelerate the recovery.

• Proper outdoor activities. We should take precautions against cold weather. Rooms should be well ventilated, and clothes and quilts should be hung out to dry in the sun. To lower the risk of infection, avoid going to public places during the flu season. Flu viruses can survive on the hands for two hours, and on hard objects such as handles and tables for 72 hours. Therefore, we must wash hands after shaking hands with others or touching possibly contaminated objects.

● Pour a 5% solution of acetic peroxide into a container, and then fumigate it naturally to disinfect the air. For a 15 sq m room you need 250ml. Change it every two days.

● Flu sufferers should avoid tiredness and ensure sufficient sleep, which helps them preserve strength, stabilize nervous and endocrine systems and improve immunity.

● Flu sufferers should follow a proper diet, with less meat and more easily digestible light food. Eat a lot of shallots, ginger, garlic and onions, since they have the effect of killing flu viruses. Vegetables rich in beta-carotene such as carrot, tomato and lucerne are also highly recommended, too. Once absorbed they convert into Vitamin A, protecting the mucosa in the nose, the throat, the bronchus and the windpipe, thus building up viral resistance. Drink more warm water or green tea, which can help dilute harmful substances in the blood, and speed up the excretion of metabolites.

● Rinse the mouth with salinated warm boiled water. Keep the body and lower limbs warm. Soak the feet in hot water for 15-20 minutes and massage the Yongquan points for two minutes before going to bed. These methods will enhance flu immunity, lessen the symptoms and accelerate recovery.

● According to research, a person's mood can influence every piece of muscle; in particular, the muscles of walls of blood vessels, medium-sized intracranial and extracranial blood vessels are highly susceptible to changes in mood. Everyone has a power inside the body which helps protect health, namely "good mood power." By optimal stimulation of the pituitary gland, a happy mood can improve hormone secretion and balance the endocrine system, which will in turn bring about a new happy mood. This virtuous circle is effective in enhancing flu immunity and speeding recovery.

● According to medical experts, the severity and duration of flu can be reduced by 20 percent by taking Vitamin C. They suggest taking two 5mg Vitamin C tablets 15 minutes after each meal, three times a day until recovery.

● This new method against flu can be practiced in conjunction with pharmacotherapy, increasing its effectiveness and accelerating recovery.

● Children must not do this on their own. They have to be guided by adults to avoid burns and electric shock.

2.2 The Simple and Effective Moxa-Stick Massage Method

This method is simple and effective, not only in the prevention and treatment of flu, but also in preventing and treating chronic bronchitis. It will help invigorate the flow of *qi* and blood, improve metabolism, microcirculation, and the function of internal organs. It is also good for the recovery of lung function, and for improving health and prolonging life as well as for beautifying the skin.

Flu and chronic bronchitis are both common diseases endangering the health and appearance of people, especially of the elderly.

Chronic bronchitis is mainly caused by bacteria, viruses and physical and chemical irritants, which will induce inflammation in the bronchial mucosa and peripheral tissue. However, the internal cause is reduced resistance of the body and the respiratory system. Therefore, the best measure for preventing and treating this disease is to strengthen the resistance of the body and the respiratory tract.

Using moxa-sticks bought from a pharmacy, the moxibustion is applied daily to selected groups of acupoints whose functions include regulating lung condition and *qi* flow and building immunity.

Group One: the Feishu (1.5 *cun* lateral to the lower border of the spinous process of the third thoracic vertebra, Fig.124); the Qihai (on the midline of the abdomen, 1.5 *cun* below the navel, Figs.125, 126); and the Zusanli (three *cun* below the lateral part of the knee and one fingerbreadth lateral to the tibial crest, Figs.127, 128).

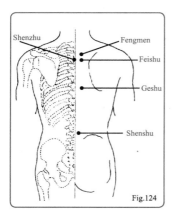

Fig.124

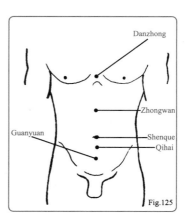

Fig.125

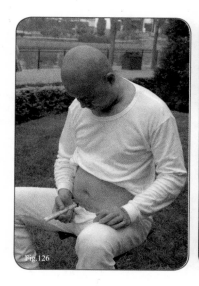

Fig.126

Fig.127

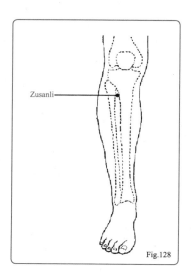

Zusanli

Fig.128

Group Two: the Dazhui (below the spinous process of the seventh cervical vertebra, Fig.129); the Geshu (1.5 *cun* lateral to the lower border of the spinous process of the seventh thoracic vertebra, Fig.124); and the Guanyuan (on the midline of the abdomen, three *cun* below the navel, Figs.125, 130).

The above two groups of points can be used in alternation. Each time needs 20-30 minutes and a course of treatment requires 30 days, with a break of three to five days between courses.

Notes:

• Prevention is the top priority for the prevention and treatment of flu and chronic bronchitis. Patients are advised to refrain from smoking and alcohol, to keep warm, have nutritious food and proper rest, and to avoid excessive sexual intercourse, cold food and cold or dusty environments.

• As the Chinese saying goes, "Get your mind healthy before starting on the body." There is an abundance of Chinese and overseas studies indicating the influence of mood upon health and treatment efficacy. Therefore, it is best to try this new method with a happy and optimistic heart.

• The above methods can be applied alone or, preferably, in combination with one or two other treatment methods.

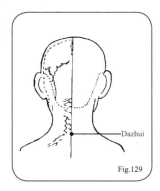

Dazhui

Fig.129

Fig.130

2.3 The Cupping Method for Prevention and Treatment

Cupping is effective not only in the prevention and treatment of flu, but also in preventing and curing chronic bronchitis. Moreover, it is good for improving health and prolonging life as well as for beautifying appearance. It is advisable to treat a group of points once every day.

Group One: the Dazhui (below the spinous process of the seventh cervical vertebra, Fig.129); the Fengmen (1.5 *cun* lateral to the lower border of the spinous process of the second thoracic vertebra, Fig.124); the Geshu (1.5 *cun* lateral to the lower border of the spinous process of the seventh thoracic vertebra, Fig.124), and the Danzhong (on the anterior midline, on the level of the fourth intercostal space, midway between the nipples, Fig.125).

Group Two: The Shenzhu (below the spinous process of the third thoracic vertebra, Fig.124); the Feishu (below the spinous process of the third thoracic vertebra, 1.5 *cun* lateral to the Shenzhu, Fig. 124); the Shenshu (1.5 *cun* lateral to the lower edge of the second lumbar vertebra, Fig.124); and the Zhongfu (one *cun* below the clavicle, six *cun* lateral to the anterior midline, Figs.131, 132).

The two groups can be used in alternation. A course of treatment consists of ten days with a break of three to five days between courses. If cupping is preceded by acupuncture with a "plum blossom" needle at the selected points, it will be more effective. Don't forget to sterilize the needle and the local skin before the treatment.

Notes:

● A marked curative effect will be attained if this method is properly applied. However, patients are advised to use it under the guidance of experienced doctors.

● In the interests of safety, exhaust cupping jars are highly recommended.

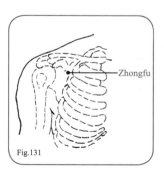

Fig.131

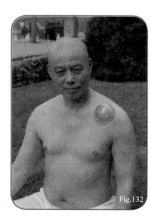

Fig.132

2.4 The Scientific and Effective Method of Salt-Pack Massage

Salt-pack massage is effective not only in the prevention and treatment of flu, but also of chronic bronchitis. This method is simple and effective. If used persistently, it will help to invigorate the flow of *qi* and blood, improve metabolism, microcirculation, and the function of internal organs. It is also good for improving health and prolonging life as well as for beautifying the appearance.

A pack consists of one kg of salt, seven slices of ginger, seven scallion stalks, and three medicinal moxa sticks. In a pan heat and stir up the ingredients to about 80°C, then put them in a piece of clean white cloth (better still, two layers of new white cloth). Bundle it with a cord. Massage the patient with the warm salt pack in the sequence and direction described below.

1. Start the massage on the back and the waist, from top to bottom and from the middle to sides (Fig.133) and to the backs of the legs, down to the feet (Fig.134), working from top to bottom. (The patient should be naked under a quilt, the massage being carried out by a family member.)

2. Massage the chest and the abdomen in the same way, from top to bottom and from middle to sides, then massage the front of the two legs from top to bottom down to the feet (Fig.135), preferably till the patient's feet perspire.

3. Apply the same massage to the inner sides of the two legs (Fig.134).

4. Massage in the same way from the chest to the hands (Fig.135), then from the hands to the shoulders (Fig.134). Then, apply the same massage to the fronts and inner sides, and to the backs and outer sides of the two arms, preferably till the patient's palms perspire.

Do this once or twice daily (the salt pack can be used repeatedly, but must be heated up first). Each massage needs 30-45 minutes. A course of treatment consists of 30 days, and there should be a break of three to five days between courses.

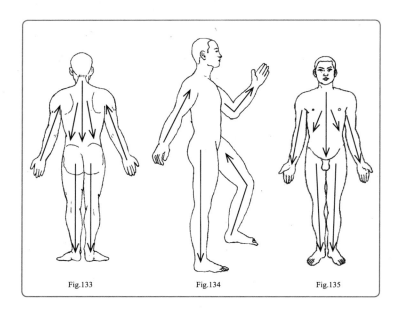

Fig.133   Fig.134   Fig.135

2.5 Effective *Daoyin* Exercise for Preventing and Treating Flu and Delaying Ageing

Daoyin exercise, which combines breathing control, body movements, mental concentration, and local massage, is a marvelous and quite unique approach, both in terms of TCM and world medicine, to preventing and treating flu and other illnesses, beautifying appearance and keeping fit. Because of its unique superiority and subtlety, possession of this precious secret has remained exclusive since ancient times, being passed on only by word of mouth. Since it has never featured on the curriculum for college students, those fortunate enough to be acquainted with *daoyin* medical science are rare indeed and those who have studied it systematically and applied it to clinical practice are even rarer. Therefore, *daoyin* has become the "lost learning" of TCM and world medicine. Now in China, *daoyin* has been marginalized, looked upon as a folk body-building method, and near to dying out totally. In 1952, I had the pleasure of getting acquainted with Yang Shaohou, the third-generation lineal practitioner of Yang-style Taijiquan. Then, I spent 50 years studying, exploring and summarizing the history, theory, prescription, method, acupoints and medical pattern of *daoyin* and its uses in prevention, clinical practice, health recovery, body-building and public health. The ten-step *daoyin* exercise described in this book not only helps prevent and treat flu, but can also replenish vigor, stabilize mood, fortify will, and prolong life.

Daoyin medicine is a dazzling pearl in the ancient treasury of Eastern occult culture. It combines breathing control, body movements and self massage, all of which can be done in the privacy of the home. It is a very effective technique for achieving a graceful figure and good looks and for improving one's immunity.

Daoyin medicine is both art and science of health and beauty. It is not only an important component of TCM, but also the quintessence of it. China's earliest medical treatise *The Yellow Emperor's Classics of Internal Medicine* describes medicine as being comprised of acupuncture, moxibustion, herbal medicine, massage and *daoyin* exercise. The first four of these approaches, all exogenous, have developed into separate disciplines. However, the unique *daoyin* medicine, kept secret by those who possessed the art, have gradually become a "lost learning," in danger of vanishing for ever.

Daoyin is culturally profound and rich, marvelously effective in preventing and treating diseases, sharpening the intellect, delaying ageing, stimulating latent immunity and prolonging life. It was highly praised by famous doctors, celebrities and philosophers of every school throughout history. However, for a variety of historical reasons, it has never risen to the theoretical foundation of modern medicine, or been recognized at the heights of modern scientific research. The *daoyin* exercises introduced here combine the advantages of Chinese and Western body-building methods, as well as past and present techniques for prolonging life. They are based on the instructions of past and present sages and the author's own research and clinical experience over dozens of years. Focusing on the problem of flu and the causes of senile decay, they include both physical and mental exercise. They are effective not only in preventing and treating flu, but also in eliminating senile plaques, protecting health and prolonging life. Exercise Seven, for instance, can not only put off ageing and prolong life, but also check and treat diseases and enhance the curative effects.

Discomfort in any part of the body or inability to complete the exercise is an indication that that part is aging (different parts of the body age at different times and vary from individual to individual). Take it in an orderly and gradual way, until you are able to complete it, and the ageing of that part will be improved. As long as you keep practicing, the curative effects will get better.

The author is glad to introduce an effective 10-step exercise for improving autoimmunity, preventing and treating flu, as well as postponing ageing and prolonging life. As long as you practice it persistently, the exercise can make you feel relaxed and refreshed, your movements flexible, and you will be able to put off ageing and enjoy a long life.

Exercise One
Concentrate the mind and get rid of distracting thoughts; regulate the breath and relax the body. (This applies to all the following exercises and will be omitted from now on. The exercises can be carried out on the floor or on the bed.) Lie on the back with the mouth and the eyes closed naturally, separate the two legs a little more than shoulder width apart and keep them straight and relaxed. Place the center of one palm on the Shenque point (navel), place the other hand on top (Fig. 136), then make rhythmical, deep abdominal breathing. (While inhaling through the nose, pull in the

Fig.136

belly; while exhaling through the mouth, relax the belly, the hands following the movement of the belly.) Repeat 16 times.

After finishing the exercise, you will feel warm and comfortable in the abdomen. It has the effects of preventing and curing flu, reinforcing original *qi*, strengthening the body and prolonging life.

Exercise Two
Close the eyes and mouth naturally and lie on the back with the arms lying either side of the body (Fig.137). Exhaling through the mouth while raising the upper body with the hands holding (or close to) the feet (Fig.138). After a few seconds, return to the original posture, inhaling through the nose (with the mouth closed). Repeat seven to nine times.

This step can prevent and treat flu, tone the liver, replenish the

Fig.137

Fig.138

kidneys, strengthen the spleen and stomach, and reduce abdominal fat. It is especially good for strengthening sexual function.

Exercise Three

Lie on the back and bend the knees. Put the elbows and the soles of the feet to the ground, shoulder width apart (Fig.139). While inhaling, raise the body, supporting it by the head, soles of the feet and the tips of the elbows; meanwhile, clench the teeth and close the mouth tightly (Fig.140). Knock the ground with the waist and the back while exhaling through the nose in snorting fashion. Repeat 16 times. Once one gets good at this, it is even more effective to support the body just with the head and feet, repeating 16 times (Fig.141).

This step helps prevent and cure flu, beautify the looks, strengthen the neck and reduce fat. It is especially good for improving muscle function in the waist, back and legs.

Exercise Four

Close the mouth and the eyes naturally and sit with the hands joined below the knees (Fig.142). While inhaling through the nose, hold the knees tightly and bring the lower jaw down to the chest as close as possible (Fig.143). After a few seconds, loosen the hands, but keep holding the knees, and throw the head as far back as possible while exhaling through the mouth (Fig.144). Hold this position for a few seconds. Repeat seven to nine times.

Fig.142

Fig.143

Fig.144

This step can prevent and cure flu, strengthen the physique, improve blood and *qi* circulation, and strengthen sexual function.

Exercise Five

Close the mouth and the eyes naturally and sit with the hands joined below the knees (Fig.142). Inhaling through the nose, hold the knees tightly, lean and lie back naturally, and roll backward till the shoulders and back of the head touch the ground (Fig.145). Exhaling through the nose, loosen the hands, but keep holding the knees and roll forward (Fig.146) to the original position (Fig.142). Repeat seven to nine times.

Fig.145

Fig.146

This helps prevent and cure flu, straighten the spine, dispel fatigue and phrenospasm, relieve pain in the ribs and activate the spirit.

Exercise Six

Kneel, with the body upright, the feet together with soles facing upwards, and hands held behind the back (Fig.147). While exhaling, sit with the buttocks on the heels; then lean the body forward till the head touches the ground (or bed), with the midpoint between the eyebrows, nose tip and navel in a straight line and focusing the attention on the navel (Fig.148). Count silently while breathing naturally eight times. While inhaling, resume the kneeling position. Repeat three to five times.

Fig.147

Fig.148

This step can prevent and cure flu, regulate the condition of the body and mind, steady the nerves and fortify the will.

Exercise Seven

Naturally close the eyes and the mouth, and kneel with the soles of the feet facing up, the arms loose on either side of the body and the palms facing inward (Fig.149). Exhaling with the nose, sit with the buttocks on the heels, then rotate the body clockwise by first leaning to the right (Fig.150) until the back of the head touches the ground (or the bed), aligning the midpoint between the eyebrows, nose tip and navel, and focusing the attention on the navel (Fig.151). Count silently while breathing naturally eight times. Inhaling through the nose, slowly raise the upper body, first lean it leftward (Fig.152) and then make the forehead touch the ground or bed (Fig.153) and resume the original position (Fig.149). Exhaling again through the nose, first sit with the buttocks on the heels and then move the body counterclockwise by first gently leaning to the left (Fig.154) and returning to the same posture of Fig.151. Count silently while breathing naturally eight times. Inhaling through the nose, slowly raise the upper body, then lean to the right (Fig.155), returning to the original posture (Fig.149). Repeat three to five times.

This step is good for preventing and treating flu, strengthening the muscles of the waist, abdomen and the legs, straightening up the body, getting rid of fatigue and activating the spirit. For those with lumbar disc herniation, it is useful in self-monitoring, treatment and enhancement of the curative effect.

Fig.149

123

Fig.150

Fig.151

Fig.152

124

Fig.153

Fig.154

Fig.155

Exercise Eight

Stand facing a wall. Stretch out the arms, with the hands parallel a shoulder-width apart and place the palms against the wall (Fig. 156). Exhaling through the nose, bend the arms outward and lift the heels. With the chest against the wall (Fig.157), slowly squat on the knees, keeping the nose tip moving down the wall (Fig.158) till the buttocks are close to the heels. While squatting, keep the nose tip and navel aligned with the midpoint between the tips of the feet. Keeping the palms in the original position, squat gradually, stretching the arms till they are straight (Fig.159). After a few seconds, inhale through the nose, slowly raising the body, and keep the nose tip moving upward along the wall, till returning to the posture of Fig.157. While raising the body, do not move the palms but crook the arms, keeping the nose tip and navel aligned with the midpoint between the feet at all times. Use the strength of the arms to return to the original posture of Fig.156. Repeat seven to nine times.

This step is effective in activating the circulation of the blood and *qi* of the whole body and improving microcirculation of the limbs. It is also good for preventing and treating flu, tackling ageing of the legs and heel pain, as well as strengthening the feet.

Fig.156

126

Fig.157

Fig.158

Fig.159

127

Exercise Nine

Stand to attention (Fig.160). Inhaling though the nose, balance on one leg and raise the other with the knee bent. Clasp the foot tightly with two hands, bringing the thigh right up against the abdomen (Fig.161). If you have difficulty in completing this you can take away one hand to support the body. After a few seconds (the longer the posture is maintained the better), exhaling through the nose, bring down the foot and return to the original posture. Then change to the other foot and practice the same movements again. Repeat seven to nine times.

This step can prevent and cure flu, as well as strengthening the legs and improving balance.

Exercise Ten

Rub the hands till they are warm (Fig.163). Then relax the whole

Fig.160   Fig.161

body by massaging in the following sequence: head, face, neck, back, waist, sacrum, chest, abdomen, arms and legs. You will feel much refreshed after the exercise (Figs.164, 165, 166).

This step can prevent and cure flu, get rid of tiredness, invigorate the brain and cheer one up.

Fig.163

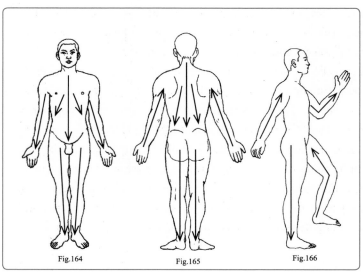

Fig.164   Fig.165   Fig.166

Notes:

• Keeping a happy mood every day is one of the secrets of longevity, and is one of the best methods of flu prevention and treatment, a self-initiated way to delay ageing and keep looking good. Therefore, in order to prevent flu and enjoy a longer life, one should have a healthy life direction, create a warm and cozy family atmosphere and build harmonious relations with others.

• One should act in accord with nature, live a regular life, have a proper diet, keep a peaceful mind, and take regular exercise. In addition, a clean living environment and good hygiene are necessary for flu prevention and treatment as well as longevity.

• According to scientists, clean faintly-alkaline boiled water at about 25°C has an affinity with the cells of the human body. It is effective for beauty therapy and health care. They suggest that adults drink eight to 10 cups (200 cc per cup) every day.

• According to biomechanics research, posture apparently exerts an influence on the individual's health and lifespan. Therefore, if we form the good habits of "standing like a pine tree, sitting like a bell, walking as fast as the wind and lying like a bow," they will help us prevent and cure flu, and enjoy a longer life.

• Leng Qian, a doctor in the Ming Dynasty, proposed 16 methods of body-building in his book *Essential Instructions for Cultivation of Longevity*. The hand-copied edition enjoyed great popularity abroad. The 16 ways were: frequent rubbing of the face; combing the hair; rolling the eyeballs; listening attentively; clicking the teeth; keeping the mouth shut; swallowing the saliva; maintaining a peaceful mind; lifting the *qi*; focusing the attention; keeping the back warm; rubbing the belly; protecting the chest; lifting and contracting the scrotum muscles; speaking sparingly; and rubbing the skin.

● Better results in delaying ageing in different parts of the body will be achieved if one performs exercises described in *Illustrated Handbook for Recuperation and Improving Appearance and Health*, based on one's own individual needs and health conditions.

● With regards to Exercise Three, patients suffering from hypertension, coronary heart disease, osteoporosis, serious rachiopathy or spinal pathology should be guided by experienced doctors; those with tumor, internal bleeding, acute inflammation, deep ulcer or serious disease should on no account do it.

Chapter 3

FLU AND THE NEW CENTURY
MEDICAL MODEL

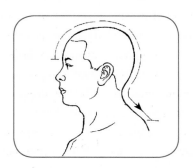

3.1 The Need for an Improved Biopsychosocial Medical Model — Ideas and Exploration of New Century Medical Model

With the publication, in 1977, of *The Need for a New Medical Model: a Challenge for Biomedicine*, the American medical scientist G. L. Engel ushered in the era of the modern medical model — the biopsychosocial model. The modern medical model marked a great stride forward, for it holds that better health and longevity in humans should be achieved through not only biological methods, but also by psychological and social ones.

At present, whether in China or abroad, in TCM, Western, mainstream, non-mainstream or integrative medicine, patients are usually considered passive receivers of treatment. Treatment of disease always concentrates on adjusting physically (or mentally) the imbalanced organism through external methods such as medication, surgery, physiotherapy and psychological consultation. These exogenous methods, which address only what is wrong, do cure the patients to some extent, but they can also bring about some toxic and side effects, such as allergy, drug-resistance, and medication dependence; some drugs such as hormones, antibiotics, and vaccines undermine the constitution, and some drugs bring about bio-functional disorder and endogenous flora imbalance in the body. According to statistics, each year approximately two million people are hospitalized due to improper medication in the U.S., and of these 100,000 die; globally, one third of all cases of illness ending in death are related to improper medication. Iatrogenic and drug-induced deaths are 10 to 15 times higher than those caused by infectious diseases in the whole world. Also, according to some research, of all the factors influencing health and longevity, inheritance accounts for 15%, social environment 10%, climate 7%, medical conditions 8%, and self-therapy (self immunity, psychological quality, lifestyle, etc.) 60%. From this it is not hard to see the importance of stressing the active, positive factors in enhancing health and longevity as well as in the prevention and treatment of flu. However, the modern medical model ignores the two positive factors that should be emphasized, namely active treatments (by patients) and passive treatments (by doctors). By contrast, the New Century Medical Model attaches great importance to these elements. It is in the guiding principles of the New Century Medical Model which aim for better patient service, to combine passive treatments (medical treatments as well as health and beauty preservation undertaken by doctors) with active ones (those undertaken by patients under doctors' instructions), and to integrate endogenous with exogenous prevention and cure, so as to help patients recover as fast and as well as possible.

The distinctive New Century Medical Model was: 1) first developed from the simple biological medical model of the past to the now commonly-applied biopsychosocial medical model; 2) it then advanced to the more scientific and rational New Century Medical Model featuring biopsychosocial treatments as well as the combination of passive and active therapy. It focuses on the essential core of future medicine — exploiting the potential of self-therapy to the fullest extent.

Active Treatments are Conducive to the Integration of Topical and Whole-Body Treatments

Active treatments attach importance to adjuvant holistic treatments (of the whole body) while emphasizing topical treatments of the affected parts, in an effort to stimulate the transformation of detrimental factors into beneficial ones in the affected parts through exploiting and enhancing the patient's overall health condition, consequently preventing and curing flu as well as reducing pain and getting rid of diseases. Its development followed the path outlined below:

WESTERN MEDICINE
Integrative medicine → analytical medicine

TCM
Holistic medicine → micro medicine

} Holistic medicine

The new holistic medicine has been achieved through the setbacks and advances of original TCM and Western medicine. Its appearance accords with the wishes of doctors and patients, as well as with the trends of social development and advances in science and technology, in medicine particularly.

According to the results of clinical research, holistic medicine (combining passive and active, endogenous and exogenous approaches), not only can enhance the curative effects of medical treatments and expand the therapeutic scope (such as beauty and health preservation), but also can help cancer patients lead a healthy life. For example, according to a research analysis report released by the scientific research department of Shanghai University of Traditional Chinese Medicine, 80% of cancer patients in Shanghai were able to lead a normal life after experiencing "integrated treatments" and "whole body recovery." From this the importance of active factors in enhancing health and longevity is quite evident.

The development of a medical model follows the rule that a given model always accords with the overall level of science and technology and of philosophical ideas in that given age. A medical model is a dynamic concept, not static and unchanging; it always develops and transforms along with the advancement of medicine. When a medical model fails to provide reasonable explanations and appropriate solutions as to changes in its scope or to new problems that emerge, of course it should be replaced by a more vital one. In fact, the New Century Medical Model not only provides further solutions to the prevention and control of diseases such as TB, STDs, and AIDS, but has also displayed significant curative effects on quite a few serious, obstinate illnesses, especially some chronic and neuropathic diseases. Furthermore, it has proved effective in helping recovery from the "sub-health" condition (or the third health condition, a state between health and illness), which has affected approximately 70% of China's population. Conventional Western medicine and TCM are unable even to diagnose the "sub-health" condition, so naturally they cannot cure it. On the other hand, effective remedies are provided by active treatments such as Chinese Taijiquan, *Qigong*, massage, *daoyin* exercise, as well as Eight Trigrams Palm, Five-Animal Exercises, Eight-Section Exercises, Form-and-Will Boxing, and Tendon-Muscle Strengthening Exercises.

According to gene theory, people are affected by flu and other diseases essentially because of disturbed gene balance. While fully confirming the positive, important effects of the biopsychosocial medical model in curing illnesses and preserving health, the New Century Medical Model also emphasizes combining passive and active, endogenous and exogenous prevention and cure, integrating this holistic approach into its guiding principles so as to rebuild gene balance and help them recover as fast and well as possible, consequently preventing and curing flu and other diseases.

Clinical observation and research results suggest that performing *daoyin* exercises under doctors' instructions is an important adjuvant method of preventing and curing flu (especially for patients affected by chronic, difficult and complicated diseases), and is a great way to enhance physiology and disease resistance, relieve pain, cure illness, and prolong life.

1. Appropriate active endo-exogenous therapy can bring about a series of significant improvements in the tissues, organs, systems, and even the whole body. Sustained *daoyin* exercises can stimulate the metabolism, consequently enhancing the functions and structures of the locomotion, cardiovascular, respiratory, digestive, and nervous systems, and stimulating the transformation of detrimental factors in the affected parts into beneficial ones through exploiting and promoting the beneficial factors of the patient's improved overall health. Undoubtedly, this will reinforce the effects of passive treatments, and be conducive to the patient's functional recovery (change from "static" to "dynamic").

2. It can replenish muscle nutrition, thicken muscle fibers, promote the proliferation of muscle cells, and enhance muscle function. Undoubtedly, this will reinforce the effects of passive treatments and be conducive to the functional recovery of paralytic muscles (especially disused ones) caused by illnesses.

3. It can enhance the flexibility and stability of joints, improve

the structures and functions of bones, help reverse detrimental pathological and physiological changes in the bones, and prevent and remedy malformation. Undoubtedly, this will reinforce the effects of passive treatments, and be conducive to recovering normal locomotion.

4. It can reallocate blood, increase hemoglobin, enhance oxygen-carrying capacity, increase the vital capacities and functions of the heart, blood vessels and lungs, and raise the state of health of the organism, as well as strengthening digestive and absorptive functions. Undoubtedly, this will reinforce the effects of passive treatments given by doctors, and create favorable conditions for the full exploitation of favorable factors in the patients' own bodies, the elevation of cell vitality, and the repair, regeneration, and functional recovery of damaged tissues.

5. It can replenish the nervous system's nutrition, adjust its conditions and enhance its functions, consequently heightening the ability of the nerve cells in the spinal cord to compensate. Undoubtedly, this will reinforce the effects of passive treatments and be conducive to recovery.

6. It can fully exploit all the positive factors in patients, enhance their belief and confidence in conquering the disease, contribute to the growth and development of their bodies (for juvenile patients), and enhance their own disease resistance (thereby inhibiting other illnesses). Undoubtedly, this will reinforce the effects of passive treatments, and be conducive to physiological and psychological improvement.

The New Century Medical Model's active endo-exogenous therapy is medically embodied in non-pharmacotherapy and exercise and behavior prescriptions featuring *daoyin* exercises under doctors' guidance. They include scientific and reasonable diet, appropriate exercises, healthy and hygienic lifestyle, healthy and balanced mentality. Hence it is not hard to see that the New Century Medical Model is economical, practical, and highly effective, one with outstanding advantages and immeasurable potential.

Active treatments also cover: 1) naturopathy such as spring therapy, and grotto, mountain, forest, fragrant flower, mud, hot sand, air, sunshine, and direction therapies; 2) physiotherapy such as color therapy, and aromatherapy, cold, hot water, magnetism, sound, wax, laser, infrared irradiation, far infrared irradiation, body frequency irradiation therapies; 3) art therapies involving music, dance, drama, calligraphy, or sculpture; and 4) entertainment therapies such as kite-flying, fishing, musical instrument, board game, and toy therapies. Furthermore, active treatments cover everything included in physical exercise therapy, acupuncture, emotion-stimulating therapy, and diet therapy.

The New Century Medical Model will also be conducive to seven major changes as regards health and life: 1) from receiving treatments only when ill to emphasizing daily health maintenance; 2) from medication-only treatments to combined medication and non-medication treatment; 3) from unitary, passive treatments to combination passive-active therapy (under doctors' instructions); 4) from death after painful illness to natural decease after a long, healthy life; 5) from disease-oriented medicine of the 20th century to health-oriented medicine of the 21st century; 6) from the current unitary, exogenous prevention and cure approach common among doctors in China and abroad, to the endo-exogenous approach of a brand new medical era; and 7) from the "biopsychosocial medical model" currently advocated energetically by the medical world in China and abroad, to the vigorous widening of the model, to feature "biopsychosocial treatments as well as the combination of passive and active ones."

Daoyin has the following features;
Daoyin, which is highlighted by the writer as one of the active treatments at the core of the New Century Medical Model, is a treasure of ancient Oriental mystery. Integrating breathing and physical exercises and self-acupoint-massage, it has proved highly effective in preserving health, youth, and beauty. It is a scientific, practical and quintessential part of oriental culture.

Daoyin, as an art of health and beauty, is highly scientific. It embodies the profound heritage of oriental medicine and culture and has many incredible effects, among them preventing and curing illnesses, awakening wisdom, preserving beauty and youth, tapping potential, and prolonging lifespan. It won the favor of great medical experts in history, for example: Bian Que, a highly skilled physician in the Warring States Period (475 – 221 BC); Hua Tuo, a renowned physician in the Three Kingdoms (220 – 280) period; Chao Yuanfang, medical erudite and minister of imperial medical affairs in the Sui Dynasty (581 – 618); and Sun Simiao, a great medical scientist in the Tang Dynasty (618 – 907); and of exponents of various schools of thought including Taoism, Confucianism, and Legalism. Unfortunately, due to limited scientific advancements, the virtuous forefathers were not able to study *daoyin* from vantage points as highly developed as those of modern medical theory or of contemporary scientific research achievements (e.g. Cybernetics, System Theory, Information Theory, Microcirculation Theory,

Holographic Biomedicine, and Senescence). In 1952, the writer was fortunate enough to meet Yang Shaohou, the third-generation lineal practitioner of Yang-style Taijiquan. Later, in an effort to make *daoyin* more scientific and systematic, the writer has spent 50-odd years in study, research, clinical practice, observation, improvements and innovation with focus on the medical method. Through this, the writer achieved some mastery of its history, theory, laws and rules, acupoints, and medical model, as well as its application in illness prevention, clinical practice, recovery, beauty and health preservation, and public health security. The efforts of more than half a century finally bore fruit.

The *daoyin* exercises of the New Century Medical Model have the following features distinguishing it from the modern medical model.

As a medical approach that is fundamentally different from the passive treatments of the current TCM and Western medicine, *daoyin* has manifested effects much more significant than passive treatments in soothing nerves and disturbed emotions, replenishing vital energy, improving blood circulation, smoothing main and collateral channels of *qi*, adjusting physiological and psychological conditions, and strengthening the viscera. It draws upon many sources and elements, for example: from India, yoga; from Japan, "Crystal Gymnastics;" from ancient Chinese *Qigong*, the valuable exhalation method with a snort through the nose, which has the effect of preventing and curing illnesses; and from Chinese martial arts, "Qigong Patting-beating," which has the effect of preserving fitness; and from modern acupoint massage for preserving beauty and health.

The features of *daoyin* are that it: 1) integrates physiology and psychology; 2) specializes in one field with various additional positive effects, and can preserve both health and beauty; 3) combines local treatments with holistic ones; 4) is rooted in TCM; 5) can be used in combination with other medical measures; 6) can be self-applied for health and beauty; 7) is economical, practical, and easy to perform; 8) has remarkable effects; 9) is applicable in a wide range of cases; 10) is highly scientific and flexible; 11) is the one and only endogenous prevention and cure method in the world; and 12) is safe and free of side effects. Daoyin, as long as performed according to the rules, is a "green" and safe medical measure to prevent and cure flu and other diseases, preserve health, beauty, and youth, and prolong lifespan. It is without any toxic or side effects, non-carcinogenic, and safe from any malformation or mutation effects.

The above advantages of *daoyin* prove that the New Century Medical Model is superior to any of its predecessors in that it is more conducive to improving medical curative effects, to widening the scope of treatment, to the complementarity of TCM and Western medicine, and to their mutual exchange, advancement and development. Furthermore, with its multiple effects — preventing and curing flu, speeding recovery, preserving beauty and health, helping with sleep and weight-loss — the New Century Medical Model is in line with current trends and future prospects in medical development.

3.2 Preventing Flu

The New Century Medical Model deals with the prevention of flu as well as all factors concerning human health and diseases. From the viewpoint of holistic medicine, it analyses in an all-around way the synergistic effect on health and disease prevention of various internal and external factors. This brand new biopsychosocial medical model not only covers the important elements of the modern medical model, but makes up for its shortcomings by combining active and passive treatments. Its core lies in the following scientific ideas and principles. First of all, we should fully affirm the effect of the biopsychosocial model in preventing flu, improving human health and treating diseases. Secondly, while dealing with influenza viruses, we should mobilize both the known and latent resistance of the body against the disease. Finally, attention must be paid to the combination of active and passive treatments, endogenous and exogenous prevention, as well as to immunotherapy, pharmacotherapy and non-pharmacotherapy. Experts have pointed out that these brand new scientific ideas and principles are of essential significance for man to usher in a new epoch of defeating flu and other diseases, and for maintaining human health and longevity.

As is generally acknowledged in Chinese and international medical circles, currently the most effective way of preventing flu is vaccination. However, although vaccination can reduce the incidence of influenza, it is still very difficult to guard against the disease because flu strains are large in number and the viruses (especially influenza A virus) readily mutate. Therefore, prevention seems more important. With a view to helping readers significantly reduce their worries and pains, I introduce below a variety of scientific and effective prevention methods, and my own invention — the Colds and Flu Prevention and Treatment Apparatus.

The Colds and Flu Prevention and Treatment Apparatus

Taking into consideration the causes of colds and flu, the author has solved the thorny problem of virus mutation (influenza A, B and C virus, especially A virus), and invented a scientific, effective and easy-to-use apparatus. It is based on repeated exploration, testing and research and over 30 years of clinical experience. It can prevent and cure influenza from the onset. Safe and without any side effects, it can directly kill the virus, mobilize the patients' own immune function with evident effect, speed recovery and bring immediate comfort. Exploiting the fact that flu viruses are temperature-sensitive and can be inactivated at high temperatures, it combines research findings from holographic medicine and the theory of meridians and collaterals. It has a marked curative effect from the onset, and is equally effective in stopping the infection spreading. The Apparatus has obtained an patent ratified by the State Intellectual Property Office of China (SIPO) (ZL 00 1 32509.4)

Compared with vaccines — he generally-acknowledged best method of prevention — the Apparatus has the following nine advantages:

1. Flu vaccines are effective only on specific viruses, but there are some 10,000 strains and mutations of flu virus, whereas the Apparatus works on all.

2. Flu vaccines have an efficacy rate of 50-90%, compared to around 95% for the Apparatus, a figure based on more than 1,000

clinical trials (on patients of 20 different nationalities) at home and abroad. Everyone feels very comfortable after the treatment.

3. Flu vaccines need two weeks to become effective, whilst the effect of the Apparatus is almost immediate.

4. Flu vaccines lose their effectiveness if people vaccinated are infected, whereas people who have used the Apparatus can continue using it post-infection, and there will be immediate relief of symptoms such as sneezing, nasal congestion, nasal mucus, cold intolerance, nausea, vomiting, fever, and severe diarrhea.

5. Flu vaccines are not right for everyone. For instance, people allergic to eggs, with heart or lung failure or serious allergic constitutions, terminal cancer patients, people in improper physical conditions or with unpredictable contraindications should not be vaccinated, and people with fever or with acute infection should delay vaccination. By contrast, any one at all, including the above groups, can use the Apparatus. At the same time, by improving microcirculation, the Apparatus can be very beneficial in recovery, beauty preserving and health cultivation.

6. Flu vaccines are costly and help only recipients of the vaccine, whereas the Apparatus costs little and can be used repeatedly by a family or a group of people.

7. Vaccines can produce side effects in people with contraindications, but users of the Apparatus would have no such misgivings.

8. Flu vaccines are prophylactic only. By contrast, the Apparatus can both prevent and cure, and can be used either alone or

with other drugs or therapies to enhance the curative effect and accelerate recovery. If used in conjunction with pharmacotherapy, it can help kill viruses.

9. The Apparatus not only resolves the divergence of views on influenza between two major schools of medical thinking in the world, but supports their correct points in every respect, making them easier to implement and popularize.

The Apparatus fills a gap both in China and abroad. The relevant departments of SIPO and Beijing Intellectual Property Office attach great importance to the patent's implementation.

Before the Apparatus finds an ideal partner and goes into production, in order to help patients tackle flu promptly and effectively, the author suggests a simple stopgap, which does not quite meet the design requirements but would not detract much from the curative effect — the hair dryer. See 2.1.

Having studied the scientific and practical flu defence and fitness measures introduced in this book, it will be plain to readers that the New Century Medical Model provides new theoretical and practical ideas that can be further utilized in the interests of better flu prevention.

Thanks to active endo-exogenous therapy, existing methods of flu prevention will surely be greatly enriched and made more effective.

3.3 Treating Flu

The New Century Medical Model deals with the treatment of flu as well as all factors concerning human health and diseases. In this dimension, as well as in flu prevention, it emphasizes the combination of active and passive, endogenous and exogenous therapies, immunotherapy, pharmacotherapy and non-pharmacotherapy.

According to gene theory, people are affected by flu and other diseases essentially because of disturbed gene balance. The New Century Medical Model emphasizes an integrated passive and active endo-exogenous therapy so as to rebuild gene balance and expedite a fast and full recovery, consequently preventing and curing flu and other diseases.

The current principles in treating flu are: to alleviate symptoms; to conserve the body's energy; to shorten the course of the disease; and to prevent complications. Can we blaze a new trail and try to find a non-pharmacotherapy that is scientific, innovative, easy-to-use, economical and without any side effects, and at the same time can directly kill flu viruses, improve blood circulation, build up resistance, speed up recovery, and effectively control influenza or stop it from spreading? This is undoubtedly a common wish.

The hot air therapy (outlined in 2.1) is based on over 30 years of the writer's personal clinical experience and research. The therapy solves the problem of virus mutation, takes advantage of the fact that high temperatures can inactivate the viruses and improve microcirculation, is in line with holographic biomedicine research and the theory of meridians and collaterals, and helps patients feel comfortable soon after the treatment.

It is well known that flu patients should take more rest and drink more weakly alkaline boiled water cooled to 25°C; this is an important adjuvant to speed recovery. In fact, any treatment effect is the result of interacting factors, namely medication (Chinese, Western or both), nutrition, psychology, and the medical model. Furthermore, besides such influencing factors as the medical environment, the quality of medical care, the experience, dedication and coordination of medical staff, and the medical model adopted, the curative effect will also be affected directly or indirectly by other factors. These include the patients' immunity, sleep, mood, confidence, self-monitoring after medication, as well as their cooperation with the doctors. Therefore, while making full use of (the doctor's) passive treatment, we should learn to adopt active and endogenous therapy as important supplementary or adjuvant therapies under the guidance of *daoyin* medicine. This is of great importance, both for enhancing the curative effects and for reducing pharmacological side effects.

Active treatment under the guidance of *daoyin* medicine can improve immunity, especially the microcirculation of the respiratory tract. Besides, it also has other advantages such as keeping fit and preserving beauty and longevity, which can be easily realized under the guidance of experienced doctors.

If we adopt active endo-exogenous therapy according to the patient's individual situation while making full use of conventional therapies, the curative effects and the medical level will undoubtedly be greatly improved.

The New Century Medical Model provides a new biopsychosocial medical model, new ideas of combining active and passive treatments, and varied supplementary or adjuvant therapies to further improve the therapeutic effect against influenza. They can either be used alone, or with pharmacotherapy, and will not only improve the curative effect but also reduce side effects.

All in all, it is of both practical and historic importance that the New Century Medical Model should point the way in combating flu. Furthermore, it will bring to the world's medical community a greater range of ideas, a broader perspective, richer content, greater flexibility, a more vigorous pace, more brilliant achievements, and more evident effects.

图书在版编目（CIP）数据

中医防治流行性感冒保健新法：英文／魏慧瑶著；
外文出版社英文编译部译.—北京：外文出版社，2009
（中国传统养生保健系列）
ISBN 978-7-119-06130-6

Ⅰ.中… Ⅱ.①魏…②外… Ⅲ.流行性感冒－中医治疗
法－英文 Ⅳ.R254.9

中国版本图书馆CIP数据核字（2009）第213950号

中医防治流行性感冒保健新法
魏慧瑶 著

选题策划　王　志
责任编辑　王　志
翻　　译　姜晓宁　李磊　曲磊　严晶　徐新歌　刘奎娟
英文审定　Sue Duncan　郁苓
装帧设计　王　志
印刷监制　张国祥

© 2010 外文出版社

出 版 人　呼宝民
总 编 辑　李振国
出版发行　外文出版社
地　　址　中国北京百万庄大街24号
邮政编码　100037
网　　址　http://www.flp.com.cn
电　　话　（010）68996140（编辑部）
　　　　　（010）68320579（总编室）
　　　　　（010）68995844（发行部）
印　　刷　北京外文印刷厂
经　　销　新华书店／外文书店
开　　本　16开（710mm×1010mm）
印　　张　9.5
装　　别　平装
版　　次　2010年2月第1版　　2010年2月第1版第1次印刷
书　　号　ISBN 978-7-119-06130-6
定　　价　75.00元